Essentials of
FORTRAN 77

Essentials of
FORTRAN 77
Second Edition

John Shelley
Imperial College Computer Centre, London, UK

John Wiley & Sons
Chichester · New York · Brisbane · Toronto · Singapore

Copyright © 1989 by John Wiley & Sons Ltd.
Baffins Lane, Chichester
West Sussex PO19 1UD, England

Other Wiley Editorial Offices

John Wiley & Sons, Inc., 605 Third Avenue,
New York, NY 10158-0012, USA

Jacaranda Wiley Ltd, G.P.O. Box 859, Brisbane,
Queensland 4001, Australia

John Wiley & Sons (Canada) Ltd, 22 Worcester Road,
Rexdale, Ontario M9W 1LI, Canada

John Wiley & Sons (SEA) Pte Ltd, 37 Jalan Pemimpin 05-04
Block B, Union Industrial Building, Singapore 2057

Library of Congress Cataloging-in-Publication Data:

Shelley, John. 1940–
  Essentials of Fortran 77 / John Shelley.—2nd ed.
    p.   cm.
  Includes index.
  ISBN 0 471 92378 8
  1. FORTRAN (Computer program language)   I. Title.   II. Title:
Essentials of Fortran seventy-seven.
QA76.73.F25S447 1989   89-33600
00513′3—dc20   CIP

British Library Cataloguing in Publication Data:

Shelley, John, *1940–*
  Essentials of Fortran 77. – 2nd ed.
  1. Computer systems. Programming languages :
  Fortran 77 language
  1. Title
  005.13′3

ISBN 0 471 92378 8

Printed and bound in Great Britain by Courier International, Tiptree, Essex

Dedication: To My Mother

Contents

Preface

This text is based on a programming course given to students and staff at Imperial College, London. It introduces the principal features of programming, as well as the essential features of Fortran 77. It is intended for those with little or no programming experience, and for those who wish to convert to Fortran 77 from some other language.

Fortran 77 is a large language. It is all too easy to confuse the novice by presenting at one time *all* the variations of a particular feature. Hence, care is taken to present in some cases just part of the total picture, Once confidence is gained with this subset, the reader may then move on to more details aspects.

To achieve this approach, the material has been organised at various levels, or *cycles* as I have called them. By following all the material at Cycle 1 and then returning to a study of material at Cycle 2 and, later, Cycle 3, readers will be able to absorb relevant aspects best suited to their own level of experience. However, those with some previous programming experience, or sufficient confidence, may ignore the cycles altogether.

In most practical courses, for which this text is intended, there is time only to present the essential features of Fortran 77. It is better to become confident in the use of this *working set* and, later, to discover the rest. Thus, we do not claim to teach all of Fortran 77, preferring, instead, to teach what is most needed. Chapter 15 points towards other, possibly useful features.

JOHN SHELLEY

December, 1988.

Chapter 1 Fundamental Programming Principles

Fundamental concepts

There are six fundamental concepts which need to be appreciated by those writing their first programs. Many programming courses and texts seldom underline these concepts, relying upon the student to discover them for themselves. Yet, those who have these emphasised at the initial learning stage benefit considerably. They are:

- a program requires data to 'work on' (process);
- a program lies inside the computer, whereas the data lies outside;
- the exact type of data* and its structure must be examined in detail before the program can be attempted;
- a program is written to be general, but seldom to be specific;
- program instructions are executed in strict sequence;
- simple programs are the best.

1. Programs process data

A computer can solve a problem provided that it is given:

- a set of instructions (a program)
- data upon which the instructions can work.

Without data, the program has nothing to process.
Without instructions, the computer cannot process data.

2. Program inside–data outside

Although a program is designed at one's desk, away from the computer, the program must eventually reside in the computer's memory. However, the data which the program is designed to process lies outside this memory and must be typed into memory from the keyboard or loaded into memory from a magnetic media such as a floppy disc. Consequently, during the execution of the program, it is necessary to have certain instructions which will cause the data to be

---

* Although 'data' is a collective term, it is common practice, if grammatically incorrect, to use it as a singular term.

brought into memory. These are called INPUT instructions (see Figure 1.1). Other instructions may then process the data.

Similarly, when results are produced, these need to be printed out by certain OUTPUT instructions. The programmer must insert both types of instructions, the so-called input/output instructions, in the correct place within the program so that they become effective during the program execution.

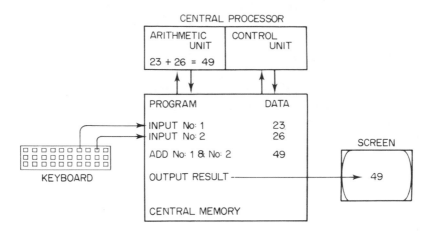

Figure 1.1

3. What type of data?

A programmer cannot write a program until the exact details about the data are known. This is not apparent when writing trivial programs. With more complex programs, however, the need to examine the data before attempting the program becomes more important.

4. Programs are general

A program is seldom written to process just one set of data. If it were, the program could be thrown aside after its first execution, since it would always produce the same results. As a simple example, a program written to input the values 4 and 5, add them together and print the result, will always produce the result of 9. If I wish to add together two other numbers, I shall need to write another program.

It is, therefore, more common for a program to be capable of adding together *any* two numbers. On one occasion, I could enter the values 4 and 5; on another I could enter two other values. This is the idea behind most programs. They are written in a generalised manner to perform the same task(s) but for many different data sets.

5. Sequential execution

When a computer stores a program in its internal memory, each instruction is placed one after the other. When told to execute the program, the computer begins at the first instruction and executes each one in turn. This is known as *sequential execution*. The only time it will *not* execute the next instruction in sequence is when the program specifically orders the computer to transfer execution to some other instruction in the program. This transfer of control operation is known as a branch, loop or jump instruction (see Figure 1.2).

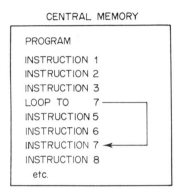

Figure 1.2

6. Keeping it simple

Many new to programming bring with them a preconceived idea that programming must be complicated. As a result, they often try to over-complicate the use of certain features. What we shall see many times in the course of this text is that keeping matters simple is the better approach. Those who avoid clever programming tricks write clear and easy to follow programs and in half the time! Always aim for simplicity rather than for cunning when writing programs.

Proverb 1
Keep it Simple, Sweetheart (KISS, for short).

Chapter 2   Programming Concepts

There is little value in labouring what follows, at this stage, despite its importance. The concepts outlined become one's own knowledge only after reflection based on solid practical programming experience. However, we all need to start somewhere. It is hoped that, by presenting the material now, you may begin to reflect on its implications as you proceed through the text and, therefore, start to appreciate the art of writing programs and why programs have to be constructed the way they are.

What is covered here are the only four basic operations computers can perform; the three processes which all programs consist of; and, finally, a brief introduction to the design of programs. To do full justice to the latter would require a separate text devoted to what is known as *programming methodology*.

Four basic operations

Computers, no matter what shape, size or cost, perform but four basic operations:

- input/output operations,
- arithmetic operations,
- movement of data operations,
- comparision/branch operations,

and that is all! Proof of this would require a computing science course. Since this is beyond our present task, it must be taken on face value. Any programming language, therefore, must permit the programmer to instruct the computer to perform these operations. Examination of any instruction in any programming language will reveal it to consist of one or more of these four basic operations. Expect, therefore, that the features of Fortran 77 discussed in the rest of this text comprise these operations.

What this implies is that the art (skill or what you will) of programming lies not so much in any complexity or richness of programming instructions, but rather in the ability of the programmer (that is you and me!) to de-compose a given problem into an interplay between these simple and fundamental computer operations. It requires a new approach to problem solving, one a beginner must acquire, and therein lies the art of programming.

These four basic functions are the simple building blocks with which more complex forms are designed. By marshalling the simple blocks into an organised form (a program), a complex problem can be solved. We gain the ability to solve complex problems by starting with simple

4

problems. This is nothing new. What is new is the approach we must take when solving problems using a computer.

Program processes

It has been proved by Bohm and Jacopini* that any program comprises only three processes:

- sequence
- choice
- repetition

Sequence: Computers execute instructions in sequence, one after the other, unless they are told to do otherwise.

Choice: This process simply tells a computer which instruction to execute next; the next one in sequence or an instruction which is somewhere else in the program.

Repetition: Computers would never have been used were it not for their ability to repeat a group of instructions time and again and at high speed. If the concept of zero is crucial to modern Mathematics and the round wheel to transport engineering, then this process of repetition is central to computing.

There are often several ways, in any programming language, to achieve choice and repetition. Some methods are more organised than others. We look further at these processes in Appendix B where we discuss structured programming.

Program plans

Another well-known proverb among the programming fraternity is:

> *Proverb 2*
> **The sooner you code, the longer it takes to program.**

Briefly, it means that you need to plan your approach before attempting the solution. The more effort put into this planning stage, the easier and quicker it is to write the program; but of more concern is the fact that good planning results in correct programs.

It is the senior programmer who plans and designs the program; it is the junior who writes the instructions. To be honest, this text teaches the skills of a junior programmer. Nevertheless, to do that job successfully, we need to be aware of some of the skills required by the senior person.

---

* C.ACM No. 5, May 1966, pp.366–71.

This whole area is a separate subject involving a study of programming methodologies, systems analysis and programming experience.

What is covered here is a method of program design based on the so-called English pseudo-code. The plan takes the form of a written English text which will eventually be converted (coded) into actual program instructions.

We use brackets to signify that what is contained within is a separate function or task. Three keywords are used: EXIT, CONTINUE and REPEAT . Where brackets are nested and one exits from an inner nest, the implication is to move back into the next higher or outer level of bracket. Finally, the design is meant to be understandable even by those with little programming experience, and to be read from the top down, like written text. Appendix A discusses these program plans in further detail. It is suggested that you read this appendix after you have gained experience with some of the Fortran features.

Chapter 3   First Acquaintance with Fortran 77

Cycle 1

Translation

A given make of computer can understand but one language, the one it was designed to recognise and obey. This is called its *machine language*. Computers, then, do not understand Fortran. Consequently, a Fortran program needs to be translated into its machine-code equivalent (known as the *object code*) before the computer can execute (obey) it. The translator of a high-level language is called a *compiler* and the translation stage is known as the compilation process. Figure 3.1 illustrates a Fortran program (the *source code*, that which is written by the programmer) being converted into object code which can then be executed by the computer.

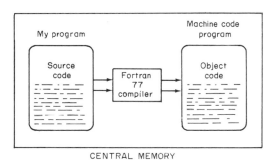

Figure 3.1

Since each make of computer has its own machine language, each computer needs to have its own version of a Fortran compiler.

Execution

Every program has to undergo two phases. The first phase is the translation stage and, provided that there are no syntax errors (mistakes in the use of the language), the object code is executed – the second stage. In Fortran, there are two statements related to both these stages: The END statement and the STOP statement. Although they seem similar, they perform different functions.

The END statement tells the compiler that there are no more instructions to *translate*. It must, therefore, be the very last statement in a program.

The STOP statement tells the computer not to *execute* any more instructions. In the early programs in this text, the STOP will appear just before the END statement. However, it can be placed at any sensible point in a program. If the STOP statement immediately precedes the END statement, the former may be omitted.

> *Tip*: It is not necessary to compile a program each time it is executed. Once you know that the program is working correctly, you may save the compiled version as a separate file. Next time you want to execute the program, you need merely execute the compiled file. This can more than halve the computer time.

The Fortran 77 character set

Each programming language tends to have its own character set, rather like natural languages. When writing program *instructions* only these characters are permitted to be used. Figure 3.2 shows those for Fortran 77. There are 50, or 49 if you prefer not to class the double asterisk as a separate character. Fortran IV has the same set, except for the colon (:). In Chapter 7, Cycle 2, we shall see why this additional character was introduced.

When typing instructions, some computers may allow lowercase characters to be used since they will be converted to uppercase by the computer system. If this is not a feature of your machine, you will have to type in uppercase.

26	letters of the alphabet:A– Z (uppercase)
10	digits: 0–9
5	arithmetical symbols: + – * / * *
9	other symbols: ( ) . = , ' $: space

Figure 3.2

Structure of a Fortran statement

Figure 3.3 illustrates the use of columns in Fortran 77. Since Fortran was the first high-level language to be developed, its structure and design go back to the days when the punched card was a major form of input to the computer. It was designed before terminals and keyboards were developed. This is reflected in the structure of the Fortran statement. The card had 80 columns and each column may now correspond to the 80 "columns" on the screen.

Columns 7–72 are used for the Fortran statement. The instruction may be placed anywhere within this area. This permits programmers to indent various instructions as an aid to readability.

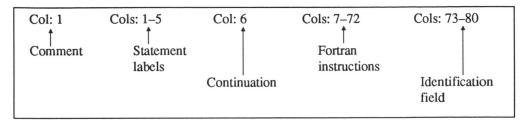

Figure 3.3

Columns 1–5 are used for statement labels (in reality, these are numbers). A label is in the range 1–99999. Labels can be typed in any of the first five columns. It is good practice to decide early on whether you prefer to left or right justify these labels and to be consistent throughout your programming career. This text uses left justification.

A letter C placed in column 1 is used to identify the remaining line as a comment, rather than a program instruction. Comments allow a programmer to document the program. We shall see how useful this can be throughout the text. The compiler ignores these lines and whatever they contain.

Column 6 is normally blank. If any character other than space (blank) or 0 (zero) is put in column 6, the compiler treats this line as a continuation of the previous instruction. This is used when an instruction would extend beyond column 72. Many programmers adopt a convention of numbering their continuation lines, either by using letters of the alphabet or numbers.

Columns 73–80 are totally ignored by the compiler. They can be used by the programmer for whatever purpose he/she decides. In the punched-card era, each card was numbered in sequence so that if the deck of cards were dropped, the programmer could reassemble the card deck in the correct order. Others used this so-called *identification field* to identify any modifications subsequently made to the program.

The following illustrates a short Fortran program. We shall examine in detail what it does in the next chapter.

```
Col:1   Col:7
            PROGRAM INOUT1
       C    This program reads in two values
       C    and outputs the same two values.
       C
            READ (*,*) VALUE1, VALUE2
            WRITE (*,*) VALUE1, VALUE2
            STOP
            END
```

Figure 3.4

The PROGRAM statement

Each Fortran program must have a name by which the compiler can identify it. This is achieved through the PROGRAM statement which consists of the reserved word PROGRAM followed by an invented name of up to six characters, using only letters and digits. This statement must be placed at the beginning of the program. In the above, the program has been called INOUT1.

If it is left out, some compilers will give the program a name; others may not bother to execute the program! Normally, one tries to make the name meaningful so that when presented with a list of program names, it is easier to identify their purpose.

Note the use of the STOP and END statements, although the STOP statement can be omitted when it appears immediately before the END statement.

Another translator of high-level languages is the *interpreter*. It is commonly used with the BASIC language. The main difference between a compiler and an interpreter is that the former will translate the *entire* program before allowing the program to be executed, whereas the interpreter will translate one instruction and immediately execute the generated code. It then moves to the next instruction, translates and executes.

The advantage of the interpreter is that when an instruction has a syntax error, the programmer can immediately correct the error and continue execution from that point. However, the execution time for programs is much slower, especially where loops (repeated instructions) are involved. Also, it is not normally possible to create a complete translated version as a separate file. Thus, interpreted languages need to be translated and executed each time the program is used.

Exercises

1. a) Explain the purpose of column 1 and column 6.
    b) Explain the purpose of columns 1–5, 7–72 and 73–80.
    c) Which columns are totally ignored by the compiler?

2. Must a program instruction begin in column 7?

3. Fill in the blanks.

    The source code is written by the ....
    The object code is generated by the ....

4. What additional character was introduced into Fortran 77?

5. Explain the purpose of the STOP and the END statements.

6. Under what circumstances may the STOP statement be omitted?

7. What is the maximum number of characters a program name may contain in standard Fortran 77?

8. Which of the following are invalid Fortran characters?

    * & } (9 o 0 " ! ? : ; B b \

Caution: Typesetting problem

Note well that some of the program instructions in the later sections are too long to fit onto one line of this text. The publisher has adopted a common practice of putting the excess onto the next line. In reality, such lines fit without problem between columns 7–72 of the display screen and would not require a continuation marker in column 6.

Likewise, not all Comment symbols (C in column 1) can be displayed in column 1 and the program instruction in column 7. To accommodate publishing limitations, it appears that the Comment symbol begins in column 1, but the instruction in column 5. Naturally, the reader will interpret this as being column 7.

Chapter 4   Free-Format READ and WRITE

Cycle 1

We shall now look at how to input and output numeric data. Remember that input instructions are the only means of getting outside data into the memory of the computer and that output instructions are the only means of displaying results produced by programs.

> Unless the program and the data are inside the main central memory, the computer cannot execute the program instructions, and the program cannot process the data.

The following program requires the user of the program to enter two numbers so that they can be stored inside the computer. Most programs would continue from this point and process the data numbers and, eventually, produce results. Here, we merely ask the computer to output these same two data values, but in reverse order.

```
      PROGRAM INOUT2
C
C Input and output 2 values.
C

      READ   (*,*) VAL1, VAL2
      WRITE (*,*) VAL2, VAL1
      STOP
      END
run              ...... to execute program
? 12.3, 25.6  ...... note input prompt [?]
25.6    12.3  ...... output from program

End of Execution ...... computer system message
```

Figure 4.1

In Fortran, the keyword which tells a computer to pause so that the user can enter data is READ. At this point, the computer stops and displays an input prompt (typically, a question mark, ?). The user enters the two numbers, separated by a comma, and presses the ENTER key (sometimes called RETURN). The ENTER key is used to mark the end of data entry. Chapter 9, Cycle 2, discusses this further under the heading *input stream*.

The purpose of the (*,*) following READ will be explained in detail in Chapters 9 and 10. But briefly, it tells the computer that the data is to come from the keyboard. It cannot be omitted, and each asterisk *must* be separated by a comma. You will have to get used to this level of detail and the use of the comma. The compiler would not allow the program to execute if the comma were left out!

What then are the two names VAL1 and VAL2? In order to appreciate this we need to digress for a moment and discuss the structure of computer memories.

The computer memory

The computer memory can be likened to a honeycomb comprising many cells. Instead of storing honey in each cell, the computer may store either a program instruction or a data item, such as a number or a series of characters (see Figure 4.2). The formal terminology for a cell is a *location* or *word*. Each location is numbered in sequence to allow the computer to locate the contents of any individual location.

0 INSTRN 1	341 23	682 AND
1 INSTRN 2	342 26	683 DOG
2 INSTRN 3	343 45.75	684
3 INSTRN 4	344	685
⋮	⋮	⋮
⋮	⋮	⋮
340 INSTRN n	681 CAT	1023

Figure 4.2

The actual number of locations will vary from one machine to another but all computers measure the number of locations in so many Ks. The symbol K stands for a *binary kilo* – 1024, not the decimal kilo 1000. Thus a 640K memory will have $640 \times 1024 = 655\,360$ memory locations. Computers always number each location, the first one starting at zero. Thus the last location in a 640K memory is numbered 655 359.

Figure 4.2 shows a 1K (1024) memory in which the locations are numbered from 0 to 1023. The number is called the *address* of the location, rather like the number of a house which forms part of its address. When a piece of data or, indeed, an instruction is required by the computer's processing unit, it looks for the address of where it is stored.

Suppose that it is required to enter two values, 26 and 24, into a computer's memory so that a program can multiply the two numbers together, produce the result and output that result. Each value entered must be stored in a separate location. But in which two locations do they go?

- we do not know!
- we do not care!
- because, we do not need to know!

The reason for this is that high-level languages use names instead of actual location addresses. If we were to write in a low-level language, then it would become necessary to specify actual addresses and this would entail keeping a record of which locations had been used and for what purpose, and which locations were still free for later use. This record keeping becomes a chore for the low-level language programmer.

High-level languages remove this chore by allowing the programmer to chose *names*. It then becomes the computer's task to keep a record of the names used and to which locations the names have been assigned. In the example program, INOUT2, Figure 4.1, the compiler will pick up the two names we have invented, VAL1 and VAL2, allocate free (unused) address locations to them, and maintain a record (log). When a subsequent reference is made in the program to one of the names, the computer searches through its records to see which address the name has been assigned to. All the programmer has to do is to remember the names chosen and the purpose for which they have been used.

Variables

The formal term for these names is *variables*. In practice, we need to keep a record of all variable names and the purpose for which they are used. If we ascribe meaningful variable names, this will help us to remember their purpose. In a long program with many variables, a name list becomes essential and, indeed, is often included at the start of the program using the C (comment) symbol in column 1. (See page 146 in Appendix A.) Variable names, then, are the means whereby we keep track of where our data is stored in main memory. In our program, the line

```
READ (*,*) VAL1, VAL2
```

will result in the program requesting the entry of two numbers into the variable names VAL1 and VAL2. These will be associated with two locations in memory into which the numbers 26 and 24 will be stored (see Figure 4.3).

26	366	601
27	367	602
28 VAL1 368 26		603
29 VAL2 369 24		604
30	370	605

Figure 4.3

Real and integer constants

Before we can consider the rules for creating variable names, we need to be aware that Fortran makes a distinction between numbers with a decimal point and numbers without a decimal point.

Integer numbers

Numbers without decimal points are called *integers*. Here are some examples:

   10 + 31 − 435 0 100123

If the sign is missing, the number is assumed to be positive. No commas or spaces are allowed within integer or real numbers.

Real numbers

A number with a decimal point is called a *real* number. Some examples are:

   0.0 .123 −.123 + 0.123 −5. −5.00 123456.123

Although 1 and 1.0 are the same value, they are two distinct entities as far as Fortran is concerned, the former being an integer value, the second being a real. They are stored quite differently inside the computer. You may think this is being somewhat pernickerity. However, Fortran deals with real and integer numbers in totally different ways. This distinction occurs in many places within Fortran syntax and, if not adhered to strictly, can be the occasion of error. So we must get used to making this distinction as well.

The values above are referred to as *constants*, real or integer constants as the case may be.

Rules for creating variable names

Because Fortran makes the distinction between integers and reals, we need to know how to create real and integer variable names.

1. Variable names have up to six characters (some extensions to standard Fortran allow seven or more). The characters may be only letters of the alphabet and digits. No other characters are permitted (except that spaces between characters are ignored!).

2. The first character of the name must be alphabetic.

3. If this first character is one of the following six letters then the variable will store its value in integer form: I J K L M N.

4. If it is not one of the above six (namely, A – H and O – Z), then the variable will store its value in real form.

If you try to store a real value in an integer variable name, or vice versa, then some form of conversion takes place. (See Chapter 5 on Arithmetic to see the implication.)

> **INTEGER/REAL/IMPLICIT** statements may be used to override these default forms; see Chapter 15.

Back to the program

```
READ (*,*) VAL1, VAL2
```

VAL1 and VAL2 are real variable names, hence the input of two real numbers. The computer has been told that there are two variables in the READ statement and it will not proceed with the next instruction until both numbers have been input. If we press the ENTER key after entering the first value, another input prompt would be displayed. (This may not be the case with every computer.)

> A Fortran compiler will always remove spaces within a program instruction. That is the way it has been designed. Consequently, a comma is required to separate one variable from another to avoid the following occurring:
>
> READ (*,*) N1 N2 ..... would become
> READ (*,*) N1N2 ...... one variable name, not two!

Writing out values

```
WRITE (*,*) VAL2, VAL1
```

The Fortran keyword to denote an output operation is WRITE. We see again the sequence (*,*). Briefly, this tells the computer to display information at the screen. Following this, we see the list of variable names. The computer will display the *contents* of the variables and in the order in which they are listed.

User-friendly comments

There is nothing more aggravating when running a program than to see the input prompt appear without any comment. We are left wondering what to input; one or more values, in real or integer form, etc.? The following program outputs comments (via the WRITE statement) to inform the user of the program what to enter. Note the comma between the comment in single quotes and the next variable name.

```
      PROGRAM INOUT3
C
C User friendly output.
C
      WRITE   (*,*)  'ENTER 2 VALUES, SEPARATED BY A COMMA.'
      WRITE   (*,*)  'FIRST A REAL, THEN AN INTEGER.'
      READ    (*,*)   REAL1, INT1
      WRITE   (*,*)  'INTEGER = ',  INT1
      WRITE   (*,*)  'REAL    = ',  REAL1
      WRITE   (*,*)  'END OF PROGRAM'
      STOP
      END

 run
      ENTER 2 VALUES, SEPARATED BY A COMMA.
      FIRST A REAL, THEN AN INTEGER.
      ?  12.34,  -55

      INTEGER = -55
      REAL    = 12.34
      END OF PROGRAM

End of Execution
```

Figure 4.4

Any comment, silly or meaningful, can be displayed along with the values held in the variable names. Each comment must be enclosed between *single* quotes (apostrophes). Any spaces inside the comment will produce spaces in the display. That is how I was able to ensure that both equal signs were aligned.

Any character that can be displayed by the computer may be entered into such a comment. We are not restricted to the Fortran character set.

> **WRITE (*, *) by itself with no variables and no comments will produce a blank line.**

Other simpler forms of I/O

```
      READ *, REAL1, INT1
      PRINT *, INT1, REAL1
```

Both these forms achieve the same result as the other READ and WRITE statements mentioned above. They also READ from the keyboard and PRINT to the screen. However, they are not so powerful as the others; we shall see why in Chapter 10.

```
      PROGRAM INOUT4
C
C Input and output 2 values using
C the simple READ & PRINT.
C
```

```
READ *, VAL1, VAL2
PRINT *, 'NUMBERS ARE: ', VAL2, VAL1
STOP
END
```

Figure 4.5

Meaningful variable names

It is the wise programmer who takes the trouble to create variable names which help him or her to remember the purpose for which the variable is to be used. TAXDED (tax deducted), NETPAY (net pay), GRSPAY (gross pay) are all meaningful variable names within a payroll program. They help the programmer to avoid using the wrong variable. Any aid which can reduce the source of errors in a program marks the professional programmer from the amateur. In complex programs, it may become necessary to provide a name list of variables, similar to an index, where each variable and its particular usage is noted. An example is shown on page 146, Appendix A.

Reserved words such as READ/WRITE/END/STOP will be accepted by the compiler as valid variable names. However, to do so is regarded as bad practice because of the inevitable confusion which will arise between what is a variable name and what is an actual instruction.

Exercises

1.   Why must the ENTER (RETURN) key be pressed to indicate the end of data input?

2.   Classify the following constants as integer, real or invalid:

1003	1,324	0.0
303.123	0.032,567,890	−87.512.62
+0012.67	.7654	0

3.   Explain the term 'variable'.

4.   Explain the significance of the first letter in a variable name.

5.   What is implied when the first letter of a variable name begins with the letters I, J, K, L, M or N?

6.   Classify the following variables as integer, real or invalid:

COST.	INT1	R3
SAVINGS	JOB NO	Kt

2ABCD	X7V56Y	TYPE 2
-GTF	K9	INK

7. What is the purpose of (*, *) in READ and WRITE statements?

8. Why should we be encouraged to use 'user-friendly' comments during program execution?

9. What is the difference between WRITE (*, *) and PRINT *, ?

10. Why is the first opening quote of a comment in a WRITE statement the same way round as the last?

11. In the following program, there are seven deliberate errors. Can you spot them?

```
      PROGAM INPUTOUTPUT
 Comment: input & output numbers.
      READ *, VAL1 VAL2
      WRITE (*,*) "VALUES = ", VAL1, VAL2
      END
      STOP
```

Figure 4.6

12. *Program Exercise 4.1: Write a program to read in two integer values and two real values and to output the real numbers followed by the two integers. Use suitable comments to annotate the input of data and the output of the values.

(Note that Program Exercises marked with an asterisk are illustrated in Appendix C.)

Chapter 5   Arithmetic

Cycle 1

Fortran was designed specifically to solve problems of a mathematical and scientific nature. We are, therefore, allowed to write expressions in a style close to algebra, thus:

$$x = a + b \qquad \text{becomes} \qquad X = A + B$$

However, as we shall see, shortly, it is a psuedo-mathematical language. We include the above *arithmetic statement* in the following program and Figure 5.2 illustrates how this is processed by the computer.

```
      PROGRAM ARITH1
      PRINT *, 'ENTER 2 REAL VALUES.'
      READ (*,*) A, B
      X = A + B
      PRINT *, A,' + ',B,' = ',X
      END
 run
    ENTER 2 REAL VALUES.
 ? -6.5, 12.5

 -6.5 + 12.5 = 6.0
```

Figure 5.1

Before execution, the compiler will note our three variable names (A, B and X) and allocate addressed locations to each one.

During execution of the READ statement, values are typed in by the user of the program and the computer stores these in the variables A and B. Once these have been entered, the computer executes the next instruction. This causes a copy of the contents of both A and B to be transferred into the Arithmetic Unit. The Control Unit tells the Arithmetic Unit to perform addition and the result is computed.

But where will the result be stored? It cannot stay in the Arithmetic Unit; it must be transferred into central memory. That is the reason for the variable X: a named location where the result can be stored after computation in the Arithmetic Unit.

Having placed the result into location X, we can now print out its contents together with relevant annotation.

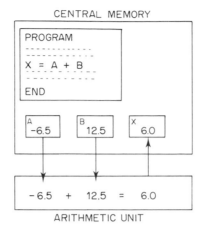

CENTRAL MEMORY

PROGRAM

X = A + B

END

A
-6.5

B
12.5

X
6.0

- 6.5 + 12.5 = 6.0

ARITHMETIC UNIT

Figure 5.2

Right v. left

There is a definite purpose for the right- and left-hand side of the so-called equals operator. The right-hand side comprises the elements (variables and/or constants) to be computed. The left-hand side is always a *single* variable name into which the result of the computation may be placed. Here we see the first example of Fortran's pseudo-mathematical nature. Both the following algebraic expressions are valid:

$$x = a + b \qquad a + b = x$$

However, if we attempt to write the second as a Fortran arithmetic statement, it will not be accepted by the compiler:

A+B = X.

This is illegal because it does not follow the rules for the right and left-hand side of the equals operator. First of all, the elements to be computed are on the wrong side of the equals operator. Secondly, the left-hand side is meant to be a single variable name to contain the single result of the computation. It is this second error which the compiler would detect. In fact, the compiler would complain about the + symbol not being a valid character within a variable name. We shall have to become accustomed to adhering *strictly* to such rules of syntax.

The assignment statement

Note that the arithmetic statement is an example of the movement of data operation; one of the four basic operations performed by computers. It is almost implicit within the instruction itself. Another and more simple example is the following, called an *assignment statement*:

```
X = Y
X = 2.3
```

In the first, we are asking for a *copy* of whatever is stored in Y to be placed in location X. The contents of Y remain unaltered. In the second, we are asking for the value 2.3 to be placed inside location X.

The value 2.3 is called a *constant*, that is, its value cannot be changed (obviously); it is fixed or constant each time the program is executed. Furthermore, it is a real numeric constant. However, Y, being a variable, can receive any value which is read into it or assigned to it many times throughout one program execution. In other words, a variable may take various values during a program execution.

```
READ (*,*) Y
......
READ (*,*) Y
```

If 728.5 were entered into Y by the first READ instruction, the next READ instruction could enter any other value into the location. The original would be destroyed (overwritten, as we tend to say). Let us suppose that 6.0 were typed in on the second occasion. We need not worry about the 72 still remaining. These digits will be written over by leading zeros:

| 0000000728.5 | becomes | 0000000006.0 |

Note the two ways of putting data into named memory locations (variable names). One is via the READ statement; the other is via an arithmetic/assignment statement. It is important to appreciate this in order to understand why certain variables need to be *initialised*, that is, they are assigned some value before being used on the right-hand side in an arithmetic statement (see Chapter 6, page 41).

Counters

The rules for the left-and right-hand sides of the equals sign allow a very useful facility, namely, a means for counting. Look at the following:

```
J = 0        ...... assignment statement
.........
J = J + 1    ...... arithmetic statement
```

The last statement breaks a fundamental law of algebra, but not of Fortran. It is a perfectly legitimate programming statement. The assignment statement assigns zero to J. The arithmetic statement places the contents of location J (0, initially) into the arithmetic unit and adds to it the constant 1. The arithmetic unit now contains 1. The rest of the arithmetic statement is simply asking for this result to be put into location J, overwriting whatever was previously there.

If we were to have some mechanism for repeating this statement and for testing for the value of J, we would have a counter! We shall see how useful this can be in the next chapter.

Points to note

Several points have been implied in the above which, for the sake of clarity, need to be emphasised.

- Variables and constants may be mixed on the right-hand side of the equals operator.
- Variables used in arithmetic statements follow the normal rules for inventing names.
- Since the right-hand side is eventually reduced to one value, no matter how complex it is, the left-hand side may contain but one variable, in which the result is stored.
- Constants are not READ into memory during execution.

Let us discuss this last point. The compiler performs several tasks:

1. Translates source code into object code.
2. Checks for the correct use of Fortran 'grammar' (syntax).
3. Issues error messages if a statement breaks the rules.
4. Assigns our variable names and constants to memory locations.

```
PROGRAM  ARITH2
WRITE (*,*) 'ENTER COST & DISCOUNT (AS A PERCENTAGE)'
READ (*,*) COST, PERCNT
DISCNT = COST*(PERCNT/100.0)
ACTCST = COST-DISCNT
AMOUNT = ACTCST+(ACTCST*0.15)
WRITE (*,*)
WRITE (*,*) 'CHARGE + VAT = ', AMOUNT
END

run
ENTER COST & DISCOUNT (AS A PERCENTAGE)
? 97.50, 10.00

CHARGE + VAT =   100.9125

End of Execution
```

Figure 5.3

We shall see how to round to two decimal places in Chapter 9. During compilation of Program ARITH2 the compiler will assign the names COST, PERCNT, ACTCST, DISCNT and AMOUNT to memory locations. It will also assign the constant 0.15 to a location (see Figure 5.4). When the program is ready to be executed, the constant is present inside memory and, consequently, there is no need to READ it in. The fact that we place constants within program instructions will ensure that they will be stored in memory prior to execution.

CENTRAL MEMORY

COST		
DISCNT		
ACTCST		
0.15 0.15		
AMOUNT		

Figure 5.4

Other arithmetical operators

The symbol + denotes addition. What we would normally call signs or symbols tend to be called *operators* in programming jargon! The other arithmetical operators are:

X = A − B	− (subtraction)
X = A * B	* (multiplication)
X = A / B	/ (division)
X = A ** B	** (exponentiation)

Order, order!

What is the correct answer, according to the laws of algebra, for the following: $X = 2 + 5 \times 4$ — 28 or 22?

Multiplication is always performed before addition, thus 22 is correct. But what order is followed in Fortran? It follows the same rules as algebra and includes expressions within parentheses. The order is this:

1.   (...)   anything within parentheses
2.   **   exponentiation
3.   *   or / multiplication or division
4.   + or −   addition or subtraction.

Some examples

X = 6 + 33 / 3	= 6 + 11 = 17
X = (6 + 33) / 3	= 39 / 3 = 13
X = 4**2 + 6 / 2	= 16 + 3 = 19
X = 3*6 + (33 − 3)	= 18 + 30 = 48

When the compiler encounters an arithmetic expression with more than one arithmetical operator, it searches first for parentheses and will perform whatever is inside. It will then drop to the next level and begin searching for any exponentiation operators ($**$). The third level is multiplication and/or division; and, finally, addition and/or subtraction.

Complex v. complicated

Before we look at how the compiler tackles expressions with more than one arithmetic operator, we need to be aware of how the computer performs arithmetic.

The arithmetic unit can perform *one* arithmetic operation (addition, subtraction, etc.) on *two* values. That is all! Consequently, an expression with more than one operator is said to be *complex* and has to be broken down into *sub-expressions* where a sub-expression consists of *one* operator and *two* values. Thus: X = A + B $*$ C is a complex expression.

This becomes: TEMP = B $*$ C   1st sub-expression
          X   = A + TEMP   2nd sub-expression

The above is by no means complicated, but it is complex. The compiler has to reduce the expression into two sub-expressions since there are two arithmetic operators. (Note that temporary variable names will be created by the compiler to contain the partial results. TEMP is used above.) A complex expression may also be complicated, in mathematical terms. As an example, let us see how the compiler will reduce the following expression:

    X = A + B/2.0**I((3.0 + 6.0) − C) + D

The compiler works from the left-hand side of the equals operator towards the right-hand side, looking for the highest level (parentheses). If there are nested (inner) parentheses, then the innermost one is evaluated first. The partial results which will occur during execution need to be stored in temporary locations. These temporary locations will be given names (of which we are totally unaware) by the compiler. Here, T1, T2,..., T6 have been chosen. The other variables, A,B,C, etc., have the values during execution as shown in Figure 5.5.

What the compiler will produce	Contents of variables during execution	
T1 = (3.0+6.0)		T1 [9.0]
T2 = (T1−C)	C [6.0]	T2 [3.0]
T3 = 2.0**I	I [2]	T3 [4.0]
T4 = B/T3	B [16.0]	T4 [4.0]
T5 = T4*T2		T5 [12.0]
T6 = A+T5	A [7.0]	T6 [19.0]
X = T6+D	D [1.0]	X [20.0]

Figure 5.5

The compiler always begins searching from left to right for the highest level. Once it has completed this pass, it returns to the left and begins searching for operators at the next level down. This process is repeated for all levels.

Notes

1. Level three gives equal status to both multiplication and division, evaluating whichever it comes across first from left to right. Thus, in our example the contents of location B is divided by whatever T3 will contain during execution. The same applies to level 4 (addition and subtraction).

2. The programmer is totally unaware of what the compiler is doing. It would not even be necessary to mention it except that it becomes crucial for a correct appreciation of *mixed mode arithmetic*, discussed below in Cycle 2.

Additional points

1. The inclusion of parentheses in expressions which do not require them does not harm such expressions. They take longer to type in, of course, but they may help to make certain expressions more readable: X = A + (B*C)

2. Use of parentheses may force a different order, should this be desirable. Thus:

    X = (A + B) * C

3. Arithmetic operators *must* always be included even though they are not always required in algebra:

    $c(a + b)$ must be written as: C * (A + B)

4. Finally, Fortran does not permit two operators to be used together, except the use of the double asterisk to denote exponentiation. Thus, Y raised to a negative 3 and A added to minus B would look like:

    X = Y ** −3   X = A + −B

But this breaks the rule! The answer is to enclose the negative in parentheses, thus: Y**(−3); now the compiler will be perfectly happy. Likewise, A+ −B must become

    A + (−B) or −B + A.

Mixing types

In Fortran, care is needed when types (integers and reals) are mixed *on either side* of the equal operator. Take the following, where [J = 4 and L = 6]:

    A = J + L

Integer 10 is computed in the Arithmetic Unit and we asking for this to be placed in a real variable, A. The integer has to be converted to real, namely, 10.0000 .... This is perfectly straightforward, but let us look at this next example:

K = A * B   where [A = 5.1 and B = 2.1]

The Arithmetic Unit computes the result as 10.71. But we are asking for this result to be placed in an integer variable K. What Fortran does is to truncate, *not* round. Thus, integer 10 ends up in K! Even if the results were to come to 10.9999, the decimal point and everything that follows is lost!

If you want the true result, take care not to mix types on either side of the equal operator!

Integer division

We now come to what some, new to Fortran, regard as a curious feature, namely, dividing by integers. Look at the following:

A = J/L   where [J = 7 and L = 3]

Using our pocket calculator, the result is shown as 2.333 recurring. But in Fortran, the Arithmetic Unit, containing two integers, finds how many whole times 3 goes into 7; the result being 2. Now we are back on familiar territory where we are asking for integer 2 to be placed in real A. Hence, A will contain 2.000.

If it is necessary to find a real result, then we need to use real division, by assigning the integer variables to real variables first, thus:

```
X = J
Y = L
A = X/Y
```

On output, A will now be written out as 2.333.

When do we need to use integer division?

Sometimes it may be necessary to separate the digits on either side of the decimal point as two individual integer values. For example, suppose that we wish to convert a given number of pence into whole pounds and whole pence so that each can be written out in separate boxes, perhaps onto an invoice form. Here, integer divison becomes useful. The following illustrates this for a data entry of 240p where it is required to print out the integer pounds into one box, and the integer pence into another box some distance away.

```
      PROGRAM INTDIV
      READ   (*,*) NPENCE
      NSTER  = NPENCE/100
      INTPNC = NPENCE - 100*NSTER
C  ... now I can write out values with spaces
      WRITE (*,*) NSTER, '        ', INTPNC
```

```
        STOP
        END
    run
    ? 240

            2                40
```

Figure 5.6

The third line illustrates integer division. 100 goes into 240 exactly 2 times. This result is placed in NSTER. Line four, according to the order of operators, multiplies 100 by whatever is in NSTER (2 in this instance), to give the result 200 which is now subtracted from the original entry of 240. This results in 40 being stored in INTPNC. Having got values in two separate locations, they can be written out with as many spaces between them as necessary. We could not do this if we had used real division!

Take care when using integer division. For example, IA = 5/3*6 results in 6, not 10, since 5/3 yields 1. On the other hand, all the following will result in the answer 10! 5*6/3; 6*5/3; 5*(6/3); (6/3)*5

Table 5.1 illustrates some mathematical notations expressed as correct and incorrect Fortran expressions.

Table 5.1

Mathematical Notation	Correct Expressions	Incorrect Expression	
$a \cdot b$	A*B	AB	(no operator)
$a \cdot (-b)$	a*(-B) or A*B	A*-B	(two operators side by side)
$-(a+b)$	-(A+B) or -A-B	-A+B or -+A+B	$(= a' + 2)$
a^{i+2}	A**(I+2)	A**I+2	
$a^{b+2} \cdot c$	A**(B+2.0)+C	A**B+2.0*C	$(= a^b + 2 \cdot c)$
$\dfrac{a \cdot b}{c \cdot d}$	A*B/(C*D)	A*B/C*D	$\left(= \dfrac{a \cdot b}{c} \cdot d \right)$
$\left(\dfrac{a+b}{c}\right)^{2.5}$	((A+B)/C)**2.5	(A+B)/C**2.5	$\left(= \dfrac{a+b}{c^{2.5}} \right)$
$a[x + b(x+c)]$	A*(X+B*(X+C))	A(X+B(X+C))	(missing operators)
$\dfrac{a}{1 + [(b/2.7 + c)]}$	A/(1.0+B/(2.7+C))	A/(1.0+B/2.7+C)	$\left(= \dfrac{a}{1 + (b/2.7) + c} \right)$

Exercises: Cycle 1

1. Explain why constants within instructions do not have to be read into memory by a READ statement.

2. Explain the purpose for the left-hand side and the right-hand side of the equals operator in an arithmetic statement.

3. Why is the following Fortran statement incorrect?   X + B = D

4. Explain the difference between an assignment statement and an arithmetic statement as given in this text.

5. If the variable X contains 3.45, what will both variable Y and X contain after the following instruction has been executed?

    Y = X + 1.2

6. What is a complex expression (where an expression is whatever appears on the right-hand side on an equals operator)?

7. The variable A contains the value 10.987. What will K contain when the following instruction is executed?   K = A

8. Swap the values in A and B without losing either value.

9. Write Fortran expressions corresponding to each of the following mathematical expressions:

    (a) $\dfrac{a+b}{c+d}$

    (b) $\left(\dfrac{a+b}{c+d}\right)^2 + x^2$

    (c) $\dfrac{a+b}{c+[d/(e+f)]}$

    (d) $1 + x + \dfrac{x^2}{2!} + \dfrac{x^3}{3!}$

    (e) $\left(\dfrac{x}{y}\right)^{g-1}$

    (f) $\dfrac{(a/b)-1}{g[(g/d)-1]}$

10. *Program Exercise 5.1: Write a program to read in three positive real numbers and to output the following:

- the three values read in,
- their sum,
- the average.

In addition you should attempt to annotate your output.

11. Program Exercise 5.2: Write a program to determine the average speed for a journey which involves going from A to B; B to C; C back to A. Use the following formula and data:

A – B: 50 miles in 2 hours

B – C: 198 miles in 3.5 hrs

C – A: 9 miles in 15 minutes

$$\text{average speed} = \frac{\text{distance}}{\text{time}}$$

In addition, compute the cost of petrol for the journey. Assume the car manages 30 miles to the gallon, at 1.70 per gallon. This exercise is discussed in detail in Appendix A, but does assume further knowledge of material in Cycle 1 of Chapters 1–8 and Cycle 2 of Chapter 9.

12. *Program Exercise 5.3: Write a program to read in the prices of three items and to output the total cost and VAT at 15%.

Cycle 2

Mixed mode arithmetic

The term *mode* means the same as type. The term *mixed mode arithmetic* refers to mixing types within a sub-expression. Please read this last sentence again! The term refers to sub-expressions and not to entire arithmetic expressions. Failure to grasp this nice point frequently leads programmers into errors.

Example a): X = A+B *L

Being complex, this will be reduced to two sub-expressions, as follows.

```
TEMP = B * L            this is mixed mode! B = real; L = integer.
X  = A + TEMP           this is not!
```

Example b): X = 6.0*(2/3)

```
ITMP = (2/3)                 not mixed mode; note integer
                             division, result = 0
X  = 6.0 * ITMP              mixed mode
```

6.0 × 0 = 0.0; thus variable X contains zero!

In mixed mode arithmetic, integer variables are converted into reals since the latter has a higher rating than the former. See Chapter 15, page 129 for further numerical types and their ratings.

Multiple exponentiation

What would you expect to happen in the following?

    X = A**B**C

There is a difference between Fortran IV and Fortran 77.

Fortran IV	Fortran 77
TEMP = A**B	TEMP = B**C
X = TEMP**C	X = TEMP**C

Because a^{b^c} is the normal algebraic expectation, Fortran 77 adopted this interpretation. Beware, then, if you are using routines written in Fortran IV where compound exponentiation is used. Of course, the issue can always be 'corrected' in Fortran IV by employing parentheses: X = A**(B**C).

```
       PROGRAM EXPO
10     PRINT *, 'ENTER VALUES FOR A,B,C'
       READ (*,*) A,B,C
       X = A**(B**C)
       Y = (A**B)**C
       PRINT *,
       PRINT *, 'A**(B**C) = ', X
       PRINT *, '(A**B)**C = ', Y
       GOTO 10
       END

  run
       ENTER VALUES FOR A,B,C
       ? 2,3,2

       A**(B**C) = 512.00001
       (A**B)**C =   64.0

       ? 2,2,4

       A**(B**C) = 65536.00001
       (A**B)**C =    256.0

       ? 3,2,2

       A**(B**C) = 81.0
       (A**B)**C = 81.0        !!!!
```

Figure 5.7

Since evaluation always moves left to right for levels 3 and 4, one needs to think twice when writing expressions. For example:

```
X = A + B - C    becomes:    TP = A + B
                             X = TP - C = [(A + B) - C]
X = A / B * C    becomes:    TP = A / B   =  a × c
                                             ─────
                                               b
                             X = TP*C
```

Intrinsic functions

Intrinsic functions are discussed more fully in Cycle 2 of Chapter 12. Some of the more common functions are listed there. Most versions (perhaps all!) will support that basic set. Many others exist, some supported by certain installations while others may not be. The way to find out which functions are available at a given installation is to ask!

Note that these instrinsic functions may be nested:

```
X = SQRT(1.0 - SIN(Y)*SIN(Y))
```

Be careful to provide the correct number of opening and closing parentheses.

An example program

It is required to find the roots of the quadratic equation:

$$y = ax^2 + bx + cx \qquad \text{using} \qquad \frac{-b \pm \sqrt{b^2 - 4ac}}{2a}$$

```
PROGRAM ROOTS
WRITE (*,*) 'ENTER 3 NUMBERS.'
READ (*,*) A,B,C
D= SQRT(B*B - (4.0 * A * C)) / (2*A)
E= -B / (2*A) + D
F= -B / (2*A) - D
WRITE (*,*) 'ROOTS ARE ', E, ' AND ', F
STOP
END
```

```
run
```

```
        ENTER 3 NUMBERS.
        ?2,3,1
        ROOTS ARE -0.5 AND -1.0
```

Figure 5.8

When translating an expression from an algebraic representation to its Fortran equivalent, we must be very careful to obtain the proper order of evaluation. For example, in the following we have two syntactically correct Fortran statements but the wrong expression!

```
E = -B + SQRT (B*B - 4.0*A*C) / 2.0*A
F = -B - SQRT (B*B - 4.0*A*C) / 2.0*A
```

What will be computed is:

$$-b \pm \frac{(\sqrt{b^2 - 4ac})a}{2}.$$

Exercises: Cycle 2

1. The following formula converts a Celsius temperature into Fahrenheit:

$$F = \frac{9c}{5} + 32$$

where F = Fahrenheit, c = Celsius.

The following are three interpretations, each of which is syntactically correct and will be allowed to execute. However, one of them is wrong; which one? Which are correct and which one would you prefer to write? CEL is a variable containing the Celsius temperature.

a) `FAH = (9/5) *CEL +32`
b) `FAH = (9*CEL) /5 + 32`
c) `FAH = (9.0/5.0) *CEL + 32.0`

2. Give the correct Fortran expressions for the following mathematical expressions:

$$x = \sqrt{y}$$

$$x = \sqrt{y + b}$$

$$x = |y - b|$$

$$x = e^{y+b}$$

$$x = \sqrt[3]{\frac{a}{b} + 2}$$

$$x = \sqrt{|y + 5|}$$

3. *Program Exercise 5.4: If the lengths of the sides of a triangle are given by the values of the variables A, B and C, then the area of the triangle can be computed from:

$$\text{area} = \sqrt{S(S - A)(S - B)(S - C)}$$

where: $S = \dfrac{A + B + C}{2}$

Write a program to calculate both S and the area.

Chapter 6   Decisions and Simple Repetition

Cycle 1

A computer will execute a series of instructions in strict sequence unless it is told to do otherwise. This chapter discusses how the programmer can tell the computer to execute an instruction which is not the next in sequence, but is somewhere else in the program. In order to illustrate this let us look at the following problem.

The problem

It is required to write a program which will convert a degree in Fahrenheit to Celsius and vice versa, and to print out the result. The user of the program will type in two items of data. The first is the temperature itself, the second will be whether it is in Fahrenheit or Celsius. To represent the second data item, it has been arranged that the user will type 1 for Fahrenheit, or 2 for Celsius. Furthermore, the program will repeat for ten sets of data.

> **For example: 50.0, 1 means 50 degrees, Fahrenheit**
> **10.5, 2 means 10.5 degrees, Celsius**

Below is a simple program plan which outlines the steps the program will need to perform.

(1) ⌈ Read in temperature & type

    IS   type = 1 (i.e Fahrenheit)

         YES ⌈ Convert to Celsius
               ⌊ Print out result

         NO ⌈ Convert to Fahrenheit
               ⌊ Print out result

⌊ Repeat 10 times from (1)

Figure 6.1

We can see in our pseudo-English code that a question is posed, namely 'Is the type equal to 1?'. *If* it is, *then* (i.e YES) the temperature read in was Fahrenheit and needs to be converted to

34

Celsius; *otherwise* (i.e. NO) the temperature read in was Celsius and needs to be converted to Fahrenheit.

This is an example of the so-called decision-making process. Once it is known which type was entered, the program can be forced to execute instructions at one of two places in the program.

In many programming languages there is a construction called IF...THEN...ELSE . It is similar to the English: 'If...then...otherwise' except that 'otherwise' is changed to the shorter word 'else' (see Figure 6.2(a)). The IF part discovers whether two values are, for example, equal. If the outcome is YES (or TRUE) the instructions following the THEN statement are executed. However, if the outcome is NO (or FALSE), the computer ignores the instructions after THEN and executes those instructions following the ELSE statement.

```
If type = Fahrenheit Then        IF (ITYPE .EQ. 1) THEN

    do conversion to Celsius         do conversion to Celsius

Otherwise                        ELSE

    do Fahrenheit conversion         do Fahrenheit conversion

End of Construction              ENDIF
```

Figure 6.2(a)   **Figure 6.2(b)**

The IF...THEN...ELSE construction

Let us look more closely at the syntax of this construction before we apply it to our problem (see Figure 6.2(b)).

After the IF keyword a logical expression is enclosed in parentheses. (We shall discuss the logical expression below. For now, it asks a question so that the outcome of NO or YES can be discovered.) Following the logical expression there is the keyword THEN. Nothing else is allowed on this line!

On the next and subsequent lines the programmer puts all the instructions that the program will execute when the answer to the logical expression proves to be TRUE (YES). There can be one or many instructions. There is no limit.

When these TRUE instructions have been completed, the programmer types the keyword ELSE on the next line, all by itself. This marks the end of the TRUE block and the beginning of the FALSE block. On the lines below ELSE, the programmer enters all the instructions which the program will execute when the answer to the logical expression proves to be FALSE (NO).

When these FALSE instructions are completed, the keyword ENDIF is typed on the next line. This marks the end of the IF...THEN...ELSE construction. In this way, when the program has decided that the answer is TRUE and has executed all the instructions in the THEN block, the program will encounter the ELSE statement. At this point, the computer will ignore the instructions after the ELSE statement and will search for the ENDIF statement. It will continue to execute instructions *after* the ENDIF statement.

If the ENDIF statement is missing, the compiler will refuse to execute the program because it is the only means it has of knowing which instruction to execute after completing the THEN or the ELSE block of instructions.

The logical expression

A logical expression must be surrounded by parentheses. It consists of two arithmetic expressions on either side of a relational operator. What is an arithmetic expression and what is a relational operator? The *arithmetic expression* is anything which can appear on the right-hand side of the equals symbol in an arithmetic statement. In other words, anything that we saw in Chapter 5. Thus:

a single variable name	e.g. NEW, I, etc.
a single numeric constant	e.g. 99, 123.45, etc.
a complex expression	e.g. (A * D - 3.4) / (F * 23.5)

The relational operator

Fortran has six relational operators. Each is expressed as two letters with full stops on either side. Each operator specifies a particular relationship (hence the term) between the two arithmetic expressions, thus:

.EQ.	equal to
.NE.	not equal to
.GT.	greater than
.LT.	less than
.GE.	greater than or equal to
.LE.	less than or equal to

Examples: IF (A .EQ. B) THEN
IF (I .EQ. 99) THEN
IF (I .GT. 99) THEN
IF (I .LE. 10) THEN
IF (A*5.0 .NE. A*D**2) THEN

Figure 6.3

The arithmetic expressions on either side of the relational operator should be of the same type, i.e. both integer or both real. Failure to adhere strictly to this dictate may lead to program errors which can be extremely difficult to trace.

Back to the problem

We can now apply this feature to the temperature conversion problem.

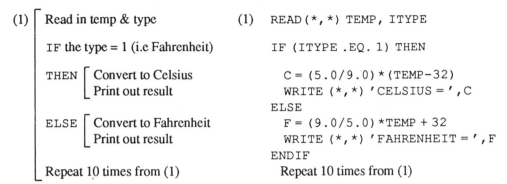

(1) Read in temp & type	(1) `READ(*,*) TEMP, ITYPE`
IF the type = 1 (i.e Fahrenheit)	`IF (ITYPE .EQ. 1) THEN`
THEN Convert to Celsius	`C = (5.0/9.0)*(TEMP-32)`
Print out result	`WRITE (*,*) 'CELSIUS = ',C`
	`ELSE`
ELSE Convert to Fahrenheit	`F = (9.0/5.0)*TEMP + 32`
Print out result	`WRITE (*,*) 'FAHRENHEIT = ',F`
	`ENDIF`
Repeat 10 times from (1)	Repeat 10 times from (1)

Figure 6.4

Note well how indenting instructions between the keywords THEN and ELSE helps to make the program more easy to read. This is good practice.

Repetition

The one thing we have not yet been able to achieve is the repetition of the program ten times. This is where the DO-loop construction will help.

DO-loop construction

The general format of the DO-loop has three parts:

(a)	(b)	(c)
Keyword	Statement number	Loop counter
DO	100	L = 1, 10

(a) The keyword DO informs the compiler that repetition is required, as well as marking the start of the loop.

```
       DO 100 L=1,10

          . . . .  ⎫
          . . . .  ⎬  instructions to
          . . . .  ⎭  be repeated

   100  CONTINUE
```

Figure 6.5

(b) The statement number (in range 1–99999) marks the instruction at the end of the loop. What has to be repeated goes in between these two.

(c) The loop counter informs the computer how many times the instructions inside the loop have to be repeated.

The loop counter

It works in this way. Initially, the loop counter variable (L in the example above, but any variable name may be used) is set to 1. The instructions inside the loop are executed. When the end of the loop is encountered (the end of loop statement number 100 above) the loop counter variable is incremented by 1. This is checked by the computer to ensure that it does not *exceed* the second value (10 in the example above). If it does not, then all the instructions within the loop are re-executed.

Eventually, when the loop counter variable does exceed the second value (i.e. L will eventually become 11), the computer will not execute the loop again, but will continue execution of the program from the instruction *after* the end-of-loop statement number.

Let us now complete our program (Figure 6.6), noting again how helpful it is to indent instructions, this time within the DO-loop as well as the IF...THEN...ELSE.

```
      PROGRAM TMPCF1
C
C A program to convert between degrees.
C

      DO 100 L = 1,10
         READ (*,*) TEMP, ITYPE
         IF (ITYPE .EQ. 1) THEN
            C = (5.0/9.0)*(TEMP-32)
            WRITE (*,*) 'CELSIUS = ',C
         ELSE
            F = (9.0/5.0)*TEMP + 32
            WRITE (*,*) 'FAHRENHEIT = ', F
         ENDIF
100      CONTINUE
      STOP
      END
```

Figure 6.6

The CONTINUE statement

The CONTINUE statement is really a 'do nothing' instruction. It is frequently used in DO-loops to mark the end of the loop by attaching to it the end-of-loop statement number as above. This practice makes it easier to see where the end of the loop occurs. Consequently, one could simply put the end-of-loop statement number on the very last instruction within the DO-loop. Thus, in our example, it would be placed alongside the ENDIF statement:

```
100   ENDIF
```

In other words, it is not the CONTINUE statement but the statement *number* which informs the computer where the end of the loop occurs!

Explanation of program TMPCF1

The first executable statement in the program is the DO-loop. During execution of this instruction, the variable L is given the value of 1. Since this does not exceed the second value 10, the instructions inside the loop will be executed. On meeting the end-of-loop statement number (100), the computer will return to the start of the loop and increment L by 1, making its current value 2. Again, the instructions are re-executed inside the loop.

After the tenth pass through the loop, L will be incremented by 1 so that it now becomes 11. Since this does exceed the value 10, the computer will pass to the instruction after the end-of-loop statement number. In Figure 6.6, this instruction is STOP. Hence the program will now stop execution.

> What would happen if someone typed in 3 as a temperature type, rather than a 1 or a 2? Since it is not 1, the program would consider it to be a Celsius type! This is not satisfactory, but read on!

Multiple choices

In the temperature conversion program there were but two choices —what to do if the type of degree was 1, what to do when the type entered was 2. However, many problems involve more than two choices. The IF...THEN...ELSE construction can be extended to cope with multiple (more than two) choices. First, let us pose a problem.

The problem: child survey program

In a child survey program for schools, part of the program has to determine how many boys and how many girls there are in each school. Let us, again, choose numbers to indicate the sex, for example, the value 1 to indicate a boy, 2 to indicate a girl. This would appear to be a case of two choices, but how would the program cope if the person entering the data typed in a value other than 1 or 2? Clearly, the user must be informed that invalid data has been entered and asked to re-input the data correctly. We now have three choices:

    1 to indicate a boy
    2 to indicate a girl
    x for an invalid entry.

For the moment, we shall assume that there are exactly 300 pupils in every school. We shall see how to cope with the situation when the exact number is not known in Chapter 8, Cycle 2.

The program plan for the survey

(1)
┌ Set counts for the number of boys and girls to zero ... (why?)
│ Read in sex code ... 1 for boy, 2 for girl
│ does sex code = 1?
│   YES [add 1 to boy count
│
│   NO ┌ does sex code = 2?
│   │
│   │ YES [add 1 to girl count
│   └ NO [print: "Invalid code, try again!"
│
└ Repeat 300 times from (1).

Figure 6.7

IF...THEN...ELSEIF

We said above that nothing follows the ELSE keyword. However, there is one exception, namely another IF...THEN statement. This allows us to discover whether another logical expression is true or false. Before coding our program, let us look at the construction in detail.

The basic structure of the IF...THEN...ELSEIF is shown in Figure 6.8.

Now we can have many choices. If the first logical expression is false, the THEN block is ignored. The computer searches for the ELSE statement and tests the logical expression following the ELSE. If this is also false, the computer moves down to the next one, and so on. If all the expressions prove to be false, then the instructions after the final ELSE (by itself) will be executed.

There is no particular limit on the number of ELSEIFs we may have. When one of the expressions is true, the instructions following the relevant THEN statement are executed down to the next ELSE. The computer will then ignore all the rest and begin execution of the instruction immediately after the ENDIF statement. (If you cover up the two ELSEIFs in Figure 6.8 you will see that it looks like the simple IF...THEN...ELSE construction.)

┌ IF (logical expression) THEN
│   ...... ⎫
│   ...... ⎬   what to do when true
│   ...... ⎭

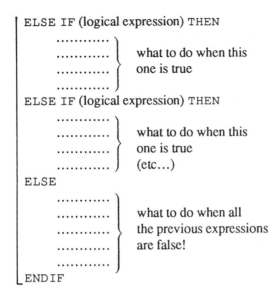

```
ELSE IF (logical expression) THEN
    ............
    ............   what to do when this
    ............   one is true
    ............
ELSE IF (logical expression) THEN
    ............
    ............   what to do when this
    ............   one is true
    ............   (etc...)
ELSE
    ............
    ............   what to do when all
    ............   the previous expressions
    ............   are false!
    ............
ENDIF
```

Figure 6.8

We can now apply this to our survey program:

```
C Child survey program:
C
      PROGRAM SURVEY
      NB = 0
      NG = 0
      DO 100 K = 1,300
          READ (*,*) ISEX
          IF (ISEX .EQ. 1) THEN
              NB = NB + 1
          ELSE IF (ISEX .EQ. 2) THEN
              NG = NG + 1
          ELSE
              WRITE (*,*) 'INVALID ENTRY, TRY AGAIN!', ISEX
          ENDIF
100   CONTINUE
      WRITE (*,*) 'NUMBER OF BOYS = ', NB
      WRITE (*,*) 'NUMBER OF GIRLS = ', NG
      STOP
      END
```

Figure 6.9

Initialisation

Why is it necessary to place zero in variables NB and NG at the start of the program? Since these two variables are to be used as counters, they need to start off at zero. Before a program is executed, some systems automatically reset every location in memory to zero. Others may put in a 'rubbish' value called an indefinite value. Others again, may do nothing so that whatever was left by a previous program will remain. If we wish to be able to run our programs on any machine, it is good programming practice to *initialise* certain variables. We then know exactly what these variables contain.

> **If a variable name is on the right-hand-side of an arithmetic statement but it has not been given a value either by a READ statement or an assignment statement, then it needs to be *initialised*.**

Variable name lists

Another good practice is to create a list of all variable names used in a program. This helps to avoid duplicating names and helps to ensure that the names are being used correctly. For our program we would create the following:

```
NB    = number of boys
NG    = number of girls
ISEX = entered sex code
      1 = boy
      2 = girl
      x = invalid.
```

Exercises: Cycle 1

1. Construct a Fortran 77 logical expression for each of the following:

    P exceeds X   Y exceeds 2.5   I is equal to J
    J is not equal to 99   K is equal to or greater than L2
    C is equal to or less than D

2. A variable N may take any of the following values, 1, 2 or 3. When N = 3, N2 becomes 0; when N = 1 or 2, N2 becomes 3.

Write a program sequence which calculates N2 for any value of N. Assume that N is given a value via a READ statement.

3. What is wrong with the following program?

```
PROGRAM ERR
READ (*,*) A,B
X = A*B*Y
PRINT *, X
END
```

Figure 6.10

4. What purpose does the ELSE statement serve in:

    a) an IF...THEN...ELSE construction
    b) and IF...THEN...ELSE IF construction?

5. Why is it good practice to indent statements within the IF...THEN...ELSE construction?

6. When should you decide to use an IF...THEN...ELSEIF construction over an IF...THEN...ELSE?

7. Explain when it is necessary to *initialise* variables.

8. *Program Exercise 6.1: Extend the program ARITH2 of Figure 5.3 to output an error message if a negative cost or percentage is entered.

Cycle 2

The Block IF

There is a shorter form of the IF...THEN...ELSE statement which may be used when there is no specific action to take when the logical expression proves to be false. In other words, the ELSE statement is not required.

```
IF (logical expression) THEN
............ ⎫
............ ⎬  what to do when true
............ ⎭
ENDIF
```

It works in this way. When the logical expression is *true*, the instructions following the THEN statement are executed. On meeting the ENDIF statement, the computer simply continues with whatever instruction follows.

However, if the logical expression proves to be *false*, the computer will ignore whatever follows the THEN statement and, since it does not find an ELSE statement, will continue with the instruction after the ENDIF.

Alternatively, we could adhere to the standard construction and simply type a CONTINUE statement after the ELSE, thus:

```
IF (logical expression) THEN
............ ⎫
............ ⎬  what to do when true
............ ⎭
```

```
ELSE
   CONTINUE
ENDIF
```

No one reading this program has any doubt that you intend nothing to be done if the logical expression is false. This approach is the one I would prefer to use since it is clearer. There is no obligation to use the CONTINUE statement. It could be omitted totally, leaving the ELSE immediately followed by the ENDIF.

Nested IFs

Entire IF...THEN...ELSEs may be nested within a THEN or an ELSE clause. But each one *must* be completed with its own ENDIF statement so that the compiler knows where each IF...THEN...ELSE construction finishes.

```
IF (log. exp) THEN             IF (log. exp) THEN
   .........                      .........
   IF (log. exp) THEN             .........
      .........                   .........
   ELSE                        ELSE
      .........                   .........
   ENDIF                          IF (log. exp) THEN
ELSE                                 .........
   .........                      ELSE
   .........                         .........
   .........                      ENDIF
ENDIF                          ENDIF
```

Figure 6.11

IF...THENs may be nested to any depth and thus extremely complex logic can be built up. This will ensure that others may find your program difficult to follow and, more than likely, you will become involved in many unpleasant hours of debugging! Keep it simple!

The Logical IF

The IF...THEN...ELSE construction was introduced into the 1977 version of Fortran. Prior to this Fortran IV programmers had access only to the logical IF statement when a choice/decision statement was required. As with most Fortran IV features, this is also available in Fortran 77. Although you will seldom need to use it, you will need to know its syntax if you have to read programs written entirely in Fortran IV. It has the general form:

IF (logical expression) a FORTRAN statement (but only one!)

If the logical expression is true, the Fortran statement on the *same* line is executed. When completed, the next instruction in sequence is executed, that is, the one on the next line.

If the expression is false, the computer moves down to the next instruction and continues execution from there. Thus, the programmer is restricted to one instruction when the expression is true.

```
READ (*,*) ISEX
IF (ISEX .EQ. 1) NB = NB + 1
IF (ISEX .EQ. 2) NG = NG + 1
............
```

This is not the case with the IF...THEN...ELSE construction in which *any* number of instructions can be written after THEN.

Note that when the logical expression is true, the statement on the same line is executed as well as the next statement in sequence (unless the GOTO statement is used). This can have undesired effects as the following illustrates:

```
IF (A .EQ. B) PRINT *, 'A = B'
PRINT *, 'A NOT EQUAL TO B'
```

Both PRINT statements will be executed when A = B! How can we avoid this? Read on!

Apart from the logical IF being a restricted statement, its worst feature is that it positively encourages the use of the GOTO. Before continuing with the logical IF, we shall need to discuss the GOTO.

The GOTO statement

This instruction tells the computer to go to another part of the program and to continue execution from that point. It does so by specifying a statement label (a number in range 1–99999). This label is then entered in columns 1–5 of the desired instruction:

```
      PROGRAM FOREVR
      WRITE (*,*) 'THIS PROGRAM WILL RUN'
15    WRITE (*,*) 'FOREVER & EVER!'
      GOTO 15
      END
```

Figure 6.12

Rules for using GOTO

1. The statement label must be a positive, non-zero and integer value in the range 1–99999.

2. The label number must be unique, that is, it can be used only once. This is reasonable because if there were two instructions with the same label, which one would the computer go to? Indeed, your program would never get to the execution stage since the compiler would detect this error.

3. You cannot GOTO a non-executable statement, for example, the PROGRAM statement (we shall meet many others before long!).

4. No numerical order is imposed on statement numbers, although it is good practice for you to impose some order to aid readability.

Logical IF and GOTO

If more than one instruction is required when the logical expression is true, a GOTO instruction is frequently necessary. It would be possible to use a SUBROUTINE (but see Chapter 11). Let us assume that we have to write the temperature conversion program using only the logical IF. One possible method is shown in Figure 6.13.

```
      PROGRAM TMPCF2
C
C     using the Logical IF
C
      DO 100 L = 1,10
          READ (*,*) TEMP, ITYPE
          IF (ITYPE .EQ. 1) GOTO 20
          F = (9.0/5.0)*TEMP + 32
          WRITE (*,*) 'FAHRENHEIT = ', F
          GOTO 100
20        C = (5.0/9.0)*(TEMP-32)
          WRITE (*,*) 'CELSIUS = ', C
100   CONTINUE
      END
```

Figure 6.13

Notes

1. An additional GOTO statement is required (GOTO 100) to avoid doing the conversion to Celsius when a Celsius temperature is read in.

2. What follows on the lines after the logical IF is what to do when the expression proves to be false and this is the opposite of the IF...THEN...ELSE construction.

What Is wrong with the GOTO?

Trying to follow the logic (flow of control) of a program peppered with GOTOs is difficult for the short-term memory. The eye has to leave the point reached and search around for the next point from which to continue. Before long, one has forgotten from where one came and what was being done. The end result is that the mind is lost in a maze of dead ends and unexplored new paths. Even the originator of the program becomes lost, let alone those who are unfortunate enough to have to grapple with the logic. Figure 6.14 illustrates the typical 'spaghetti bowl' program created by GOTOs.

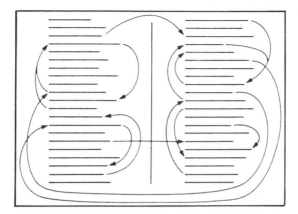

Figure 6.14 The 'spaghetti bowl' program

The use of too many GOTOs is the mark of the amateur. It leads to the most appalling confusion with the inevitable plethora of bugs. One of the main reasons for introducing structured features, such as the IF...THEN...ELSE, was to eliminate, as far as possible, the uncontrolled use of the GOTO. Indeed, at least one programming language, dBASEIII, has no GOTO statement at all! Appendix B discusses structured programming and suggests when it is permissible to use the GOTO.

The GOTO is known as the *unconditional* branch (jump, loop) instruction because the computer is forced to move unconditionally to another point in the program. There is no choice. The IF...THEN...ELSE construction (and the logical IF) force the computer to move to another point in the program only when a certain condition (as specified by the logical expression) becomes true or false. It is, therefore, known as the *conditional* branch instruction.

Logical operators

```
IF (ISEX.EQ.1 .OR. ISEX.EQ.2) THEN ......
```

The .OR. including the periods on either side is a logical operator and may be used within IF statements. On either side of the logical operator there must be a *complete* logical expression.

```
IF (logical exp. .LO. log. expression) ......
```

Thus the following would be invalid:

```
IF (ISEX .EQ. 1 .OR. 2) ......it should be:
IF (ISEX .EQ. 1 .OR. ISEX .EQ. 2) ......
```

Each logical expression is tested to see whether it is true or false. Depending on the outcome, the entire expression becomes true or false and the computer will execute the relevant series of instructions.

In the case of the .OR. either one of the logical expressions needs to be true for the whole to be true. Furthermore, *both* expressions may also be true, and not merely either one or the other as the English meaning usually implies!

In the case of the .AND. *both* expressions must be true for the whole to be true. If either is false, the whole is false. We could amend the child survey program to include a logical operator.

```
      DO 100 L = 1,10
          READ (*,*) ISEX
          IF (ISEX .NE. 1 .AND. ISEX .NE. 2) THEN
            PRINT *, ISEX, 'INVALID ENTRY, TRY AGAIN!'
          ELSE IF (ISEX .EQ. 1) THEN
            NB = NB + 1
          ELSE
            NG = NG + 1
          ENDIF
  100 CONTINUE
```

Figure 6.15

> We have now met three sets of operators. I promise there are no more.
> The first set included the arithmetic operators: + - * / **
> The second set included the relational operators: .EQ. .GT. etc.
> The third set included the logical operators: .AND. .OR.

Exercises: Cycle 2

1. Construct Fortran 77 logical expressions for the following:

   K is less than L and K is greater than M
   M is equal to J or M is greater than 6*7
   R is equal to D and F is not equal to T or W is less than F

2. Explain why the GOTO is called an *unconditional* branch instruction whereas the IF...THEN statement is called a *conditional* branch instruction.

3. There are three types of operators: arithmetic operators, relational operators and logical operators. Under what circumstances would each be used?

4. Suggest two reasons for the logical IF being a limited form of a conditional branch instruction.

5. If the Fortran statement after the logical IF but on the same line is not a GOTO statement, what does this imply when the logical expression is true?

6. Study the following program carefully and attempt a program design. See Appendix C for a solution.

```
      PROGRAM ROOTS2
      WRITE (*,*) 'TO STOP PROGRAM, ENTER 3 ZEROS'
100   READ (*,*) A,B,C
      IF (A.EQ.0 .AND. B.EQ.0 .AND. C.EQ.0) THEN
          WRITE (*,*) 'END OF PROGRAM.'
          STOP
      ELSE
          D = (B*B) - (4. * A * C)
          IF (D .LT. 0) THEN
              WRITE (*,*) 'NO REAL ROOTS.'
          ELSE
              D = SQRT(D) / (2.0*A)
              E = -B / (2.0*A) + D
              F = -B / (2.0*A) - D
              WRITE (*,*) 'ROOTS = ', E, ' AND ', F
          ENDIF
      ENDIF
      GOTO 100
      END
 run
      TO STOP PROGRAM, ENTER 3 ZEROS
      ? 2,3,1
       ROOTS = -0.5 AND -1.
      ? 1,2,3
       NO REAL ROOTS.
      ? 0,0,0
      END OF PROGRAM
```

Figure 6.16

7. *Program Exercise 6.2: It was Hero, a mathematician of ancient times, who gave us the following formula: if *a,b,c* are three side lengths, then the area is

$$\sqrt{S(S-A)(S-B)(S-C)} \quad \text{where S is the half perimeter } (a+b+c)/2.$$

A property of Hero's formula is: if $S(S-A)(S-B)(S-C)$ is negative, then *a,b,c* cannot make the sides of a triangle.

Extend Program Exercise 5.4 to determine whether the three sides entered make a triangle. If not, then output an appropriate message; otherwise, output the area of the triangle.

Cycle 3
More about logical operators

There are five logical operators in Fortran 77 – .AND., .OR., .NOT., .EQV. and .NEQV. (The last two were added to Fortran 77.)

They may be combined in any logical order within a conditional instruction:

```
      IF (A.EQ.B .AND. D.GT.E .OR. F.LE.G ......)
```

The .NOT. operator merely reverses or inverts the value of whatever follows. Thus: .NOT.(A.EQ.B) negates/inverts the value within parentheses. If (A=B) is true, the logical result of .NOT.(A.EQ.B) becomes false; if (A=B) is false, the result of .NOT.(A.EQ.B) becomes true.

The .EQV. and .NEQV. represent logical equivalence and logical non-equivalence respectively. For example:

```
IF(((A.EQ.B).EQV.(C.EQ.D)).AND.((E.EQ.F).NEQV.(G.EQ.H)))
THEN ...
```

means that if (A=B) is equivalent to (C=D) (that is that *both* are either false or true) *and* (E=F) is not equivalent to (G=H) (that is that they cannot both be true or false) then the whole is true.

Note how the logical concepts are becoming quite complex when combining logical operators. We should not forget, however, that "Keeping it Simple, Sweetheart!" is better than being too clever. The following provides the truth tables for these five logical operators.

Table 6.1

Logical Exp. A	.LO.	Logical Exp. B	Logical Result
-	.NOT.	True	False
-		F	T
T	.AND.	T	T
T		F	F
F		T	F
F		F	F
T	.OR.	T	T
T		F	T
F		T	T
F		F	F
T	.EQV.	T	T
T		F	F
F		T	F
F		F	T
T	.NEQV.	T	F
T		F	T
F		T	T
F		F	F

Let us now look at the complete order of precedence for all operators.

Priority levels

1. sub-expressions in parentheses
2. exponentiation
3. unary minus
4. multiplication/division
5. addition/subtraction
6. relational operators (all equal priority)
7. .NOT.
8. .AND.
9. .OR.
10. .EQV./.NEQV.

NOTE

The unary minus is the negation symbol. Since it falls below exponentiation, care must be taken with expressions such as: $-A ** 2$. This would be evaluated as though it had be written as $-(A**2)$ instead of $-(A) ** 2$.

Exercises: Cycle 3

1. Explain why we should not over-complicate logical expressions.

2. According to the order of precedence, EQV is lower than OR. In the following, explain why EQV is evaluated before OR.

```
IF(((A.EQ.B) .EQV. (C.EQ.D)) .OR. (A.NE.F)) THEN ......
```

Chapter 7 Subscripted Variables

Cycle 1

By inventing variable names, we can store a numeric value or one or more characters into *single* locations inside main memory. See Figure 7.1 where the variable names –RVAR; RES – have been assigned by the compiler to individual memory locations. Data may be 'stored' in these names either by a READ statement or by an assignment statement:

```
READ (*,*) RVAR
RES = RVAR * 3.5
```

Sometimes it becomes convenient to group together (consecutively) a certain number of memory locations. The purpose of this chapter is to explain how this can be achieved.

Lists

In Figure 7.1, locations 9–13 have been grouped together to form what looks like a list. We are all familiar with making lists, for example, a shopping list, a list of student names in a class, indeed, a list of numbers upon which some computation can be performed. In programming jargon, a list is more formally called an *array*. We shall discuss in Chapter 8, Cycle 1, when it becomes necessary for a programmer to create arrays.

1	8	15	22	
2	9	16	23(RVAR)	
3	10	17	24(RES)	
4.	11	18	25	
5	12	19	26	
6	13	20	27	
7	14	21	28	

Figure 7.1

What is an array?

Figure 7.2 shows a group of six memory locations all with the same name, IARRAY. Each element in the array contains an integer value. In order to refer to any single member/element in the array, we need some method of identifying it. Mathematicians would use subscripts to do this, but Fortran has no means of writing subscripts. In our array, the elements are numbered from 1 to 6. Fortran identifies an individual array element by putting the would-be subscript within parentheses and after the array name. Thus: IARRAY(3) will refer to the third element in the array, IARRAY, namely the value 56. This so-called *subscripted* variable may be used in any Fortran statement in exactly the same way that an ordinary single variable is used.

IARRAY (1)	32
(2)	45
(3)	56
(4)	12
(5)	78
(6)	44

Figure 7.2

```
READ (*,*) IARRAY(3)
M = IARRAY(3)
PRINT *, M, ' = ', IARRAY(3)
```

Figure 7.3

The subscript, also known as an *index*, is not restricted to being an integer constant; it may also be an integer variable. Clearly, this variable must be given a value *before* the subscripted variable can be used.

```
K = 6
M = IARRAY(K)*3
```

Rules for subscripted variables

1. Array names follow the normal rules for naming variables.

2. The subscript/index must be an *integer* constant or variable. Fortran 77 permits zero, negative and positive subscripts, Fortran IV allows only non-zero and positive subscripts. We shall see how to create negative and zero subscripts in Cycle 2.

3. If the array name is integer, all numeric values will be stored in integer format. If the name is real, all numeric values will be stored in real format.

4. If an array name is used, the index must always be appended. This implies that at any one time only one element of an array may be referenced. (There a few occasions when the subscript may be omitted. For example, when an array is passed as an argument in SUBROUTINEs, or in a PRINT/WRITE statement; but see Chapter 11 and Chapter 8 respectively.)

5. An array name cannot be used subsequently as a single variable name. Once it is defined to be an array, it must always remain an array name.

Allocation of memory to an array

It is the DIMENSION statement which informs the compiler how many memory locations to assign to an array. The DIMENSION statement must come after the PROGRAM statement but before any executable instruction. It is an example of a non-executable instruction which supplies the compiler with relevant information.

> Note that it is not permitted to GOTO the DIMENSION statement during execution, thereby creating an array during the execution of a program. Some languages do permit this, but Fortran does not.

```
DIMENSION IARRAY(6)
```

is the statement which informs the compiler to set aside six consecutive locations all with the same name of IARRAY. Any reference to this array within an executable instruction must have a subscript in the range 1–6. This range is called the *bounds* of the array. If a subscript exceeds the bounds, unpredictable results will occur; see page 56, Cycle 2.

If more than one array is required by a program, multiple DIMENSION statements may be used, or the arrays may be included in the same statement, separated by commas, thus:

```
DIMENSION IARRAY(6), ARRAY1(30), ARRAY2(1000)
```

Here, three arrays are being created. The number of elements in each is placed within parentheses.

Cycle 1 of the next chapter makes use of an array.

Exercises: Cycle 1

1. Which are valid forms of subscripts in Fortran IV?

```
A(-3)    MANNO(5.0)    AREA(MINIMUM)    JOB NO(1 0)
```

2. Store the tenth member of array `ALIST` into the single variable `STORE`.

3. Interchange values in `A(3)` and `A(4)` without losing either value.

4. Write one statement which will multiply the `I`th member of array `A` by the `I`th member of array `B` and store the result in the `I`th member of array `X`.

5. What is the purpose of the `DIMENSION` statement and where must it be placed in a program?

6. Why is it that an array cannot be created during run-time?

Cycle 2

Zero and negative subscripts

It was mentioned in Chapter 3 that the colon was the only character to be added to Fortran 77. It was included so that negative and zero subscripts could be used. In the following,

```
DIMENSION IARRAY(1:6)
```

the array, `IARRAY`, is again dimensioned to six locations and the subscripts may take only the values of 1–6. The number on the left of the colon supplies the starting value of the range; the number on the right of the colon supplies the maximum value of the range. This rule allows us to do the following, where again, six elements are being reserved:

```
DIMENSION IARRAY(0:5)
```

Now the subscripts may be 0, 1, 2, 3, 4, 5. Likewise:

```
DIMENSION IARRAY(-2:3)
```

Here, we again reserve six locations but the subscript may now be one of only the following: $-2, -1, 0, +1, +2, +3$.

Subscripts as expressions

Subscripts may also be arithmetical expressions either within the `DIMENSION` statement or within an array reference:

```
DIMENSION X(1:3*6)    range is 1–18
READ (*,*) X(3*5)     reference is to element 15
```

```
Y = X(5*I/J)                    reference depends on evaluation
```

In the last example, the element being referred to depends on the result of the arithmetic expression within the parentheses. Great care should be taken to ensure that it does not fall outside of the range 1–18 as defined by the DIMENSION statement.

Note that since the subscript must be an integer value, the following would fail because a real value would result:

```
IF (X(3*A) .EQ. 0.0) THEN
```

However, we could use the INT function:

```
IF (X(INT(3*A)) .EQ. 0.0) THEN ...
```

Note the balance of parentheses: three open, three closed!

Exceeding bounds

The values used in the DIMENSION statement determine the number of locations to set aside for the array as well as the range or bounds of the subscripts. We may use less than the number of elements reserved, but we should not exceed the range. For example, in the following, A has 60 locations, B has 30:

```
DIMENSION A(60), B(1:30)
...............
K = 61
Y = A(K)*115.0
```

What will happen in the above? There is no 61st element of array A. The compiler will not detect any error and so the program will be allowed to execute. It will be during run-time that the problem will occur.

What actually happens will depend very much on the type of run- time system being used. Unless we have intimate knowledge of the run-time system, we cannot be sure what will transpire. Some systems will check a subscript each time it is used to ensure that the subscript is within the valid range. If it is not, the run-time system will abort the program and generate a run-time error message. This is kind, but it does mean that the program will take longer to execute.

Other systems do no checking at all! They will quite happily convert the address of A(61) to a location somewhere in memory, perhaps, to the first location of the array B or some other location depending upon the mapping algorithm. Your program will process the value in this location to generate an erroneous result of which you may or may not become aware!

The first type of system is useful when testing your program. The second is useful (if you have the choice) when you are satisfied that all is working correctly. When used with real-live data, the second system will execute programs more quickly.

Many systems permit a TRACE facility to be used when running programs with arrays in them. The trace will list the subscript being used (arithmetic expressions being evaluated to integer constants) and the user can visually check each index.

Two-dimensional arrays

The arrays discussed so far are one-dimensional arrays. A two-dimensional array takes the form of a matrix (see Figure 7.4), and is created as follows:

RA

1,1	1,2	1,3	1,4	1,5
2,1	2,2	2,3	2,4	2,5
3,1	3,2	3,3	3,4	3,5
4,1	4,2	4,3	4,4	4,5
5,1	5,2	5,3	5,4	5,5
6,1	6,2	6,3	6,4	6,5

Figure 7.4

```
DIMENSION RA(6,5) or DIMENSION RA(1:6,1:5)
```

Either DIMENSION achieves the same result. The first number (or pair if the colon is used) tells the compiler how many *rows* the matrix is to have; the second number (or pair) tells how many *columns* there are. It is important to remember that the rows come first, so if you have any difficulty in remembering, think of Roman Catholics (RCs) or some similar mnemonic. Here, we are setting aside 6 × 5 (30) locations all with the name RA and all values in the matrix are, therefore, of type real.

Two-dimensional arrays can consume many memory locations, so be sure you calculate correctly. Thus:

```
DIMENSION IAR(100,100)... i.e. 10,000 locations,
```

Within instructions, the two-dimensional array is used in the same way as the one-dimensional array. Again, just one location can be referenced at any one time.

```
READ (*,*) A(4,2)          4th Row, 2nd Column.
A(1,2) = 23.50             1st Row, 2nd Column.
```

Three and more dimensions

Fortran allows up to seven dimensions. The third dimension adds planes to the two-dimensional matrix, as shown in Figure 7.5. It is dimensioned as follows:

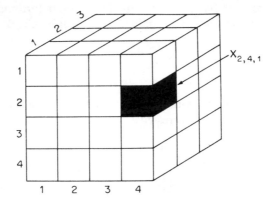

Figure 7.5

```
DIMENSION X(4,4,3)
```

Here we have 4 rows, 4 columns and 3 planes. X(2,4,1) references row 2, column 4, plane 1.

Dimensions 4 onwards are left to the imagination of the programmer; perhaps a fourth dimension could be made to represent a number of cubes or three-dimensional arrays. To be honest, I have never seen a program which uses any dimension higher than 4, although my effort to find one has been remarkably low.

Exercises: Cycle 2

1. Explain the term "array".

2. Explain the function of the colon in a DIMENSION statement.

3. Why is it important never to step out of the bounds of an array, established by the DIMENSION statement?

4. Using a PRINT statement, write out the value shown in the matrix below (Figure 7.6).

5. What DIMENSION statement would be required to create the matrix MATXYZ?

6. In the following statement, how many locations in total are being reserved for the various arrays?

```
DIMENSION X(-9:-3), Y(1:20), K(-1:9,0:5)
```

7. Given the above DIMENSION statement, why are the following subscripts invalid?

```
X(3)   X(0)   Y(1:8)   K(0,-1)
```

MATXYZ

		10,36	

Figure 7.6

Chapter 8   DO-Loops/Repetition

Cycle 1

The DO-loop construction allows repetition to be performed in a controlled manner. It is frequently used for input and output of data as well as for the manipulation of arrays. We have already discussed the basic form of the DO-loop in Cycle 1 of Chapter 6. Let us now look at a simple example with the use of an array. We need to read into an array TEMPS twenty temperatures, to compute the average and to print out all those values greater than the average.

```
      PROGRAM AVTEMP
      DIMENSION TEMPS(20)
      TOTAL = 0.0
C
C     read in and total 20 readings
C
      PRINT *, 'ENTER 20 TEMPERATURES'
      PRINT *, '1 AT A TIME!'
      DO 100 J = 1,20
         READ (*,*) TEMPS(J)
         TOTAL = TOTAL + TEMPS(J)
100   CONTINUE
C
C     compute average and print result
C
      AVG = TOTAL/20.0
      PRINT *, 'AVERAGE TEMPERATURE = ', AVG
C
C     now find those above average.
C
      DO 200 K = 1,20
         IF(TEMPS(K) .GT. AVG) PRINT *, TEMPS(K)
200   CONTINUE
      STOP
      END
```

Figure 8.1

Explanation

Having initialised TOTAL to zero, the DO-loop loop counter variable (J) is set to 1. The instructions inside the loop are executed, thus the READ statement requests the user to enter the

60

first temperature reading into the array TEMPS. Note how the loop counter variable J can be used as the subscript for the array. Each time the loop is executed, J is incremented by 1. Thus, the first value read in is stored in the first element of TEMPS; the second reading into the second of TEMPS; and so on. Each successive repetition of the loop stores the next value entered into the next element of array TEMPS.

Likewise, when totalling the temperature readings into the variable TOTAL, J is again used as the subscript.

When the DO-loop has repeated itself twenty times, the program continues with the execution of those instructions after the end- of-loop statement number (here, 100). The average is then computed and printed out.

The second DO-loop finds those temperatures greater than the average and prints them out.

Use but do not alter!

It is most important that you realise the purpose of the loop-counter variable. It is used by the computer to control the number of repetitions of the loop. Therefore, it is forbidden for the program to alter its value within the loop itself. We can make *use* of its value, but we cannot *alter* its value. The following would be forbidden:

```
DO 200 J = 1,30
   READ (*,*) X(J)
   ..............
   J = J+1
   ..............
200 CONTINUE
```

Figure 8.2

Full form of the DO-loop

In practice, the full form of the DO-loop is:

DO nnnnn loop var = m1,m2,m3

where:
nnnnn	= the end-of-loop statement number (in range 1–99999)
loop var	= loop-counter variable
m1	= starting value of loop variable
m2	= ending value of loop variable
m3	= the increment of loop variable for each pass.

If m3 is omitted, the default increment becomes 1. The three m-values may be constants and/or variables. Here are some examples:

```
DO 100 L = 1,20,1  identical to DO 100 L =1,20
```

Here, L takes the initial value of 1, to a maximum of 20 and is incremented by 1 for each execution of the loop.

```
DO 200 M = M1, M2, M3
```

Here, M takes the initial value of whatever is contained in variable M1, to the maximum contained in M2, and is incremented by the value stored in M3.

```
DO 300 N = 2,20,2
```

Here, N takes the initial value of 2, up to 20, and is incremented by 2 for each execution: 2,4,6,8,10,..., 20, i.e. 10 executions. Now study Figure 8.3.

```
      DIMENSION TEMPS(20)
C
C     Total odd elements of array TEMPS
C
      DO 100 L = 1,20,2
         TOTODD = TOTODD + TEMPS(L)
100   CONTINUE
C
      Total even elements of array TEMPS
C
      DO 200 L = 2,20,2
         TOTEVN = TOTEVN + TEMPS(L)
200   CONTINUE
```

Figure 8.3

In the first DO-loop, the variable L takes values: 1, 3, 5, 7, 9, 11, 13, 15, 17, 19.

On completion of the tenth execution, L will be incremented by 2 to become 21. This is tested against the maximum 20, found to be greater and, consequently, control will pass to the instruction after the end-of-loop statement number 100.

In the second DO-loop, L takes values: 2, 4, 6, 8, 10, 12, 14, 16, 18, 20. When it is given the value 22, control passes to the instruction after 200.

When to use an array

Look again at program AVTEMP. If it were not required to find those numbers above the average, the array would not be necessary, as we can see in Figure 8.4.

Arrays are used to store values which are required for some later processing which needs to 'look back' at each value. In the above program segment, what is stored in the single variable TEMP, once the DO-loop has completed its repetitions is the very last value read in. Each READ

(*, *) TEMP overwrites the previous value of TEMP. It is not possible to go back and view any of the previous values. To do so, would require an array.

```
      DO 100 J = 1,20
         READ (*,*) TEMPS
         TOTAL = TOTAL + TEMPS
 100  CONTINUE
C
C     compute average and print result
C
      AVG = TOTAL/20.0
      PRINT *, 'AVERAGE TEMPERATURE = ', AVG
```

Figure 8.4

Generating random numbers

RANF ( )* is a function which returns a value between 0 and 1 but never actually zero or one. Note the presence of the null argument surrounded by parentheses. The complier requires the empty brackets in order to distinguish between the number generator function and a random variable name called RANF invented by the programmer. Here are some examples of the use of the RANF ( ) function.

X = RANF ()	stores a random number in X
Y = RANF () *50.0	stores in Y a random number between 0.0 and 50.0
K = RANF () *50.0+1	stores in integer K a number between 1 and 50 and possibly including 1 and 50.

The following illustrates the creation of an array of integer random numbers, between range 1 and 100 and possibly including both. Note that the real value is truncated when stored in NARY !

```
      DIMENSION NARY(20)
      DO 100 L=1,20
         NARY(L)  = RANF()*100.0+1.0
 100  CONTINUE
         PRINT *, NARY
```

Figure 8.5

The PRINT statement will output all values in the array NARY. The computer will print as many values on one line as it can. Note that this use of the array does not require a subscript, indeed, it cannot have one since just one element would be printed. Since NARY has been dimensioned as an array, the compiler will not confuse it with a single variable name.

---

* RANF ( ) is specific to CDC CYBER machines. Other systems have RAN or RANDOM but they all achieve the same effect.

> Unfortunately, on some machines RANF() always produces exactly the same 'random' numbers in exactly the same order. This can become boring. The solution is to change the starting seed of RANF( ) so that a different set of numbers is produced. This is achieved by RANSET(X) which must be CALLed as a subroutine before invoking RANF( ). Chapter 11 discusses subroutines. RANSET is given an argument (X in the above) which must be whole, real and odd, for example, 35., 23., etc. The user can be invited to enter a new starting seed and, thereby, generate a new set of random numbers:
>
> ```
>          PRINT *, 'ENTER SEED, WHOLE, REAL and ODD.'
>          READ *, Y
>          CALL RANSET(Y)
>          . . . . . . . . . . . . . . . .
> C     generate 20 values in range 50-100
>          DO 100 I = 1,20
>          NUM(I) = RANF()*50.0+50.0
> 100 CONTINUE
> ```

Figure 8.6

Exercises: Cycle 1

1. What is the primary purpose for using a DO-loop?

2. The DO-loop counter variable may take on three different settings (m1, m2 and m3 in this text). Explain the purpose for each.

3. If the third setting (m3) is omitted, what does this imply?

4. The DO-loop counter variable may be *used* but not altered.

(i) Why is this?
(ii) Suggest one use for the DO-loop counter within the loop.

5. In the following program segment, what error has been committed?

```
     DIMENSION A(20)
     TOTAL = 0.0
     DO 100  L=1,30
        READ *, A(L)
        TOTAL = TOTAL + A(L)
 100 CONTINUE
```

Figure 8.7

6. *Program Exercise 8.1: Write a program to read in exactly six numbers, find their total and average and to output these results. You do not need an array for this program, but you will for the next.

7. *Program Exercise 8.2: Extend the above program to output all the values read in and to print those numbers less than the average.

8. Program Exercise 8.3: Write a program to generate and print out ten integer random numbers in the range 1–40.

Cycle 2

Nested DO-loops

Any valid Fortran statement may be inside a DO-loop, including another DO-loop. In this way we can nest DO-loops inside each other. However, an inner DO-loop must be completely inside another; they are not allowed to overlap. See Figure 8.13 at the end of this chapter.

Nested DO-loops form a convenient method of handling arrays of two or more dimensions. Let us suppose that it is necessary to sum each element of the array A2 of Figure 8.8, row by row. The following code will do this.

```
      PROGRAM SUM
      DIMENSION A2(7,9)
      TOTAL = 0.0
C
C     sum all elements of array A2, row by row.
C
      DO 200 J = 1,7
        DO 100 K = 1,9
          TOTAL = TOTAL + A2(J,K)
100       CONTINUE
200     CONTINUE
      PRINT *, 'TOTAL = ',TOTAL
      END
```

Figure 8.8

The loop counter variable J takes on the initial value of 1 and the instructions inside the loop are executed. The first instruction is another DO-loop, giving the loop counter variable K the value of 1. Both J and K are 1 and when used as subscripts refer to row 1, column 1. The first element is added to TOTAL. The end-of-loop statement number, 100, forces control back to the *inner* loop so that K becomes 2, whilst J remains at 1. The element A2(1,2) is now added to TOTAL. This continues until K exceeds 9, whereupon the inner DO-loop ceases and control passes to the instruction after 100.

This instruction is the end-of-loop for the *outer* DO-loop. Consequently, J is incremented by 1 (to become 2). The loop is executed again. This re-executes the inner loop setting K to its initial value of 1. Now, the subscripts refer to A2(2,1), in other words to the second row. This row is added to TOTAL, one element at a time.

A small change would allow us to add up the elements column by column. The following does this and also prints out the total for each column. Note that the column total (COLTOT) needs to be re- set to zero within the outer DO-loop.

```
        DIMENSION A2(1:7,1:9)
        DO 200 K = 1,9
           COLTOT = 0.0
           DO 100 J = 1,7
                COLTOT = COLTOT + A2(J,K)
  100      CONTINUE
           PRINT *, 'COLUMN ',K, ' TOTAL = ', COLTOT
  200 CONTINUE
```

Figure 8.9

Exit before maximum reached

So far, all our DO-loops have been executed exactly the number of times as specified by the maximum value (m2) in the loop counter. In many situations, the programmer may not know the exact number of times a loop needs to be executed. As an example, it is required to read in an unknown number of temperature readings and to calculate and print the average.

Somehow, the program needs to know when there are no more readings to be entered. There are four possible methods and these are referred to in Chapter 14, page 125, under the heading 'Detecting End of Data'. We shall choose the following method for our present problem. We simply get the user to type in a special value and when the program reads in this value, the program will 'know' that the last valid data has previously been entered.

The choice of this special number is important. It clearly cannot be a value which could ever form one of the valid readings. Since we are entering temperatures, we should know the possible range that these temperatures could take and those which are impossible. Say that the range could be anywhere between $\pm100°$ C. Now it is a simple matter to choose a reading for our end-of-data marker, say $-999°$ C. We see a possible set of data, including the end-of-data marker, below:

12.04, 23.5,$-$10.0, $-$99.10, ..., 54.65,$-$78.5, $-$999.0

When the program reads in $-$999.0, it will know that the last valid data item ($-$78.5, above) has been entered. It can then move to another part of the program and continue with the computation of the average.

```
        TMPTOT = 0.0
        DO 100 L = 1,200
           READ (*,*) TEMP
           IF (TEMP .LT. -998.9) GOTO 20
           TMPTOT = TMPTOT + TEMP
           NREADS = L                      ..... ???
  100 CONTINUE
C now compute and print average
  20  AVGTMP = TMPTOT/NREADS
        PRINT *, 'AVERAGE TEMP = ', AVGTMP
        .................
```

Figure 8.10

There are several issues worth discussing in the above code.

1. Note the use of the logical IF and the GOTO to exit the loop before the maximum number of repetitions has been reached. We could have used the IF...THEN...ELSE construction but for once it does not look so neat (see Figure 8.11). Furthermore, I always think it is a pity to put a GOTO into a construction specifically designed to avoid its use. The matter is personal, so feel free to disagree!

```
      DO 100 L = 1,200
         READ (*,*) TEMP
         IF (TEMP .LT. -998.9) THEN
            GOTO 20
         ELSE
            TMPTOT = TMPTOT + TEMP
            NREADS = L
         ENDIF
100   CONTINUE
```

Figure 8.11

2. The only way to exit a DO-loop before the maximum number of repetitions has been reached is through the GOTO statement attached to a conditional branch instruction. Incidentally, advocates of structured programming features (except the most pure) are prepared to tolerate GOTOs provided that they jump forward (down) into the program. If the GOTO forces control back up the program, then some form of repetition construction is implied and should be used.

3. Control will pass to statement 20 when the GOTO 20 is executed. The DO-loop will cease to be re-executed.

4. Finally, why is the comparison .LT. -998.9 rather than .EQ. -999.0? It is important to know that some real numbers cannot be stored exactly in binary format. For example, 0.2 decimal has no exact binary equivalent. Consequently, it is a dangerous practice to compare two real values for equality. Rather, compare for some acceptable compensation. Here, -998.9 is quite all right.

Accuracy of real numbers

It is not always possible to store real numbers exactly in the internal binary number system as used in computers. Even in decimal, this is not always possible. For example, $1/3 = 0.3333...$. Regardless of where we stop, we shall never have an exact representation of 1/3. There will always be a small but distinct truncation error. If we now perform a computation using this truncated value, the results will also have a slight error in the last decimal places.

Consequently, we should never expect a real value to be exactly equal to a particular quantity. This means that we should never test real values for exact equality. Taking the above, we cannot assume that:

$1/3 + 1/3 + 1/3 = 1.0.$

> If we need to test for equality, we must test for a value *very close* to the desired value
> and one which our program can tolerate, for example:
>
>   IF (X .GT. 0.9999) THEN

How many repetitions were made?

We need to know how many repetitions of the READ statement were made in order to have a value with which to compute the average. We have seen earlier (Chapter 10, Cycle 1) that a simple counter could be used to count the number of repetitions. But cannot the loop variable be used instead? It is being incremented by one each time the loop is re-executed. So why is it assigned to another variable, NREADS, within the DO-loop? This raises an interesting issue which we discuss next.

The problem is nothing to do with Fortran but with the particular computer one is using. We must accept that, while the DO-loop is being executed, the loop-counter variable plays a strategic role. It is used by the computer system to work out whether another execution of the DO-loop is required. That is why we are not allowed to change its value within the DO-loop. However, what happens to the variable once the DO-loop is no longer active?

Here lies the problem. We cannot be sure what a given computer system will do. Some will keep the value as it stood; others will have incremented it by 1 in preparation for the next possible pass; others again re-set the variable to an indefinite value.

Since we cannot be sure what will happen, the best thing to do is to assign its value to some other variable within the loop and make use of that variable outside of the loop. That is why the loop-counter variable has been assigned within the loop to NREADS. It can now be used quite freely, and it is certain to contain the *correct* number of loop executions.

However, the placing of the assigment within the loop is crucial. What mistake would occur in the following code, given a data set as follows: 23.0, 34.0, 45.0, − 999.0 ?

```
      DO 100 L = 1,200
         NREADS = L
         READ (*,*) TEMP
         IF (TEMP .LT. -998.9) GOTO 20
            TMPTOT = TMPTOT + TEMP
 100  CONTINUE
 20   AVGTMP = TMPTOT/NREADS
```

Figure 8.12

Three valid data readings exist and one end-of-data marker. In order to detect the − 999.0, a fourth READ needs to be executed. Since NREADS = L is placed *before* the IF, its value will be 4 outside of the loop. Whereas, if it is placed anywhere *after* the IF statement, NREADS will contain only the number of repetitions relating to valid data readings! Its value would be 3.

Other forms of Fortran 77 DO-loops

1. DO 100 L = 1,20,1 is equivalent to DO 100 L = 1,20

2. DO 200 K = 2,20,5

Here, K begins at 2, until it exceeds 20, and is incremented in steps of 5: 2, 7, 12, 17. The next increment (22) exceeds the maximum.

3. DO 300 M = 20,3,-5

Here, M takes values 20, 15, 10, 5. Zero being less than 3 stops further executions.

4. DO 400 X = 1.5, 2.7, 0.1

Here we have a real loop counter variable, X. It takes the following values: 1.5, 1.6, 1.7, ... ,2.6, 2.7. In this case, the DO-loop should be executed 13 times but it may execute only 12 times. Care needs to be taken when a real variable is used as a loop counter in DO-loops. We discuss why this is so, after a digression about trip counts.

Trip counts

The trip count is a term used to describe the number of times a DO-loop can be executed and it will always be converted into an integer form. The algorithm, using m1, m2 and m3 as described in the full form of the DO-loop, is the following:

$$(m2 - m1 + m3) / m3$$

Thus, DO 100 L = 5,20,3 becomes: $(20 - 5 + 3)/3 = 18/3 = 6$ trips. L takes values: 5, 8, 11, 14, 17, 20.

Real loop counters

Taking the following: DO 100 X = 1.5,2.7,0.1, we have:

$$(2.7 - 1.5 + 0.1) / 0.1 = (1.2 + 0.1) / 0.1 = 1.3 / 0.1 = ???$$

It should be 13.00, that is, 13 trips once it has been converted into integer. It is important now to realise that trip counts are *always* converted to integer form even though real variables are used. However, some real numbers which have fractional parts cannot always be held exactly inside the computer's memory, unlike integer values. Thus, since real arithmetic is involved, the result of the final division could be 12.999..9. When this is converted to an integer value to get the trip count, truncation will result and make the trip count 12 instead of 13!

Care must be taken when using real variables in the loop counter. It is advisable to add a small compensation to m2, say 0.05, to avoid any possible error. Thus: DO 100 L = 1.5, 2.75, 0.1

$$(2.75 - 1.5 + 0.1) / 0.1 = 1.35/0.1$$

will lead to a trip count of integer 13 without any problem!

Nested loops

Figure 8.13 shows the legal and illegal forms of nesting as well as the illegal entries to DO-loops. No matter how desirable an instruction inside a DO-loop may be, one cannot jump into a DO-loop without going through the DO-loop statement.

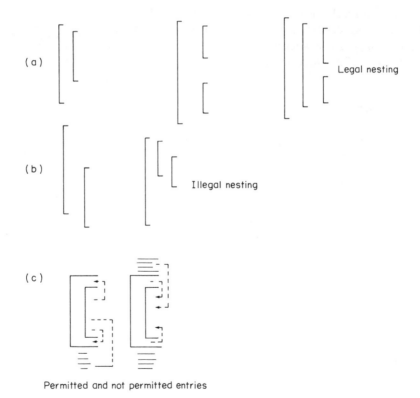

(a)   Legal nesting

(b)   Illegal nesting

(c)

Permitted and not permitted entries

Figure 8.13

Exercises: Cycle 2

1. What is the only method of exiting from a DO-loop before the maximum number of repetitions has been reached?

2. Why is the logical IF, rather than an IF...THEN...ELSE, a neater form of exit from a DO-loop before the loop has completed its maximum number of repetitions?

3. Trip counts are always calculated by the computer in integer form. True or false?

4. Why do we need to be careful when using real DO-loop counter variables?

5. Suggest one use for nested DO-loops.

6. Suggest two uses for the DO-loop counter variable within the DO-loop.

7. *Program Exercise 8.4: Amend Program Exercise 8.2 of Cycle 1 to enable an unknown number of values to be read in rather than the fixed set of six. How will you cope with finding the average?

8. *Program Exercise 8.5: Write a program to calculate and print out the total values for each row and column of a three by four matrix.

Chapter 9 FORMATted READ and WRITE

Cycle 2

If you require more control over the *exact* positioning of information on the screen or printed paper, you need to become embroiled in the use of FORMAT statements. Be warned that this can be a time-consuming exercise!

In this chapter, we discuss how to read in data which has been organised by someone other than ourselves, and look at how to format output. We discuss the latter first.

FORMATted output

```
      WRITE (*,32) IVALUE
  32  FORMAT (I3)
```

In place of the more familiar asterisk, we have put in a statement number (32). This number is also attached to a FORMAT statement. The FORMAT statement is another example of a non-executable statement and, consequently, we cannot GOTO it. In order to 'execute' a FORMAT statement the relevant WRITE (or READ) statement needs to be executed.

FORMAT statements may be placed at any point within the executable statements and before the END statement. They do not have to follow immediately after the relevant WRITE or READ. Some programmers like to place all of them at the end of their programs, whereas others prefer to have them near the WRITE/READ statements. It is the statement label in the WRITE which marries up a particular WRITE statement with a given FORMAT statement.

The FORMAT statement

Each FORMAT statement must have a unique statement label in the range 1–99999. The keyword FORMAT is placed in column 7 onwards and what appears between the parentheses specifies how the information is to be displayed. In the above example, we are writing out the value in the integer variable IVALUE. In the FORMAT statement we have the characters I3.

The I refers to the fact that an integer value is to be printed. The 3 after the I tells the computer the number of positions or places on a line in which the value is to be printed. Because it is the first item in the FORMAT statement, it refers to the first three positions on the current print line.

Thus, if IVALUE contains 123, these three digits would be printed out in the first three positions. If IVALUE contained the value 12345, then the I3 would have to be changed to I5. Then the digits would be printed out in the first 5 positions.

```
32    FORMAT (I5)
```

The parentheses must be used. The last one means that we are not interested in the remainder of the output line and that nothing else is to be output on that line.

The general format is:

```
nnnnn FORMAT (Iw)
```

where: nnnnn   = a label in range 1–99999
          FORMAT = the keyword for the statement
          I   = that an integer value is to be printed
          w   = the width or number of positions for the value.

All Fortran reference manuals use the symbol w to denote width.

If more than one value is to be printed, each one must have its own Iw, known as an *edit descriptor*, thus:

```
         WRITE (*,1000) IVAL1,IVAL2,IVAL3
 1000    FORMAT (I3,I5,I7)
```

If   IVAL1 contained   [123]
      IVAL2   [12345]
      IVAL3   [1234567]

The following would be produced:

123123451234567

making it somewhat difficult to read. To get some spaces between numbers we use the X symbol, where nX specifies how many spaces. If three spaces were required between each number, I would type:

```
 1000    FORMAT (I3,3X,I5,3X,I7)
```

   123   12345   1234567 would result from the above.

If I wish to include a comment within my output, the comment must be enclosed in single quotes, as before, but now I can place it within the FORMAT statement, thus:

```
1000 FORMAT ('THE NUMBERS ARE: ', I3,3X,I5,3X,I7)
```

   THE NUMBERS ARE: 123   12345   1234567

If it is necessary to output only a heading and no values, for example, column headings, type:

```
      WRITE (*,22)
 22   FORMAT (10X,'HEADING A',15X, 'HEADING B')
```

```
HEADING A                 HEADING B
```

Note

Each item in the FORMAT statement must be separated by a comma. Note also that the w follows the I (I3), whereas the number of spaces precedes the X (3X)! If you get this the wrong way around, the compiler may not execute your program.

> When using FORMAT statements you may need to decide whether to output for a screen (which has 80 positions/columns per line) or computer paper (which may extend between 65 and 136 positions; 120 is quite common).
>
> Note also the built-in redundancy in the FORMAT statement. Despite the fact that we are printing the contents of the integer variable IVALUE, we must still inform the compiler via the Iw that IVALUE is integer.

Writing out REAL numbers

We had to specify that an integer value was to be output. Likewise, we need to specify in the FORMAT statement that a real value is to be output. The symbol used for reals is F, standing for the other name for a real value, namely, floating point.

```
      X = -0.09
      WRITE (*,30) IV1,REAL1,X
 30   FORMAT (I5,3X,F7.3,3X,F5.2)
```

Figure 9.1

The general form is: Fw.d where:

$$F \;=\; \text{indicates a real value}$$
$$w \;=\; \text{the maximum number of printing positions, as with Iw}$$
$$d \;=\; \text{number of significant digits } after \text{ the decimal point.}$$

Make sure that you really understand the purpose of 'd' above! Suppose REAL1 contains the following value inside the memory of the computer: $-12.122657\ldots$. F7.3 states that the value is to be printed in the next 7 positions with the number of significant digits after the decimal point rounded to 3, so -12.123 will be printed.

Do *not* assume that F7.3 means nnnnnnn.nnn! F12.3 would be required.

In the w field we need to include room for the minus sign (if it exists) and for the decimal point. The number of characters, then, in -99.999 is 7: 5 digits, 1 minus sign and 1 period.

Bearing this in mind, the w should always be at least 2 greater than the d. `W>=d+2`.

What happens when a variable to be output contains less digits than specified by the w field? For example, see the following:

```
IV1     contains     123
REAL1   contains     123.455678...
IV2     contains   12345
REAL2   contains   12345.12345....
```

The FORMAT however states:

```
      WRITE (*,55) IV1, REAL1
 55   FORMAT (3X,I5,3X,F9.2)
      WRITE (*,55) IV2,REAL2
```

Figure 9.2

Fortran prints out values in the specified w field from right to left. Any positions which are not used are filled with blank spaces. (In this way, decimal points always align neatly!) In the following, ^ will stand for a blank space so that you can count them. The above FORMAT will cause the output to look like:

```
^^^^^123^^^^^^123.46
^^^12345^^^^12345.12
```

Note that multiple WRITE (and READ) statements may use the same FORMAT statement.

But what occurs if the w field is too small? A seven-digit number cannot be squeezed into a four-character w field. Exactly what will happen during run-time depends on the particular computer system being used. Most will print out some special character (e.g. an asterisk) in the number of positions specified by the w. This will draw the programmer's attention to the fact that he/she will need to increase the w field.

FORMATted READ

When reading data from a keyboard with a FORMATted READ, it is not permissible to put commas within the w field. The reason for this is that the computer expects to find numeric data in the w field and objects when it finds non-numeric data, such as a comma.

The input stream

The input stream is whatever is typed in after the input prompt (including spaces) and before the RETURN key is pressed. If a comma falls into a w-idth group, it will be rejected as being a non-numeric character. In the following program, three items of data need to be entered into variables I, J and K. The input stream is also shown. Since commas are present, we must tell the computer to ignore them by taking the trouble to insert the relevant 1Xs.

```
      READ 30, I,J,K
 30   FORMAT(I2,1X,I2,1X,I2)
      .....................
?12,34,45
```

Figure 9.3

The point is, why bother with a FORMAT statement in the first place? Just use free-format.

The Iw in the FORMAT statement informs the computer that an integer value is to be input and to look for that value within the first w positions, 5 in the example below. The I3 in the same FORMAT statement forces the computer to look in the next three positions for the second value. Consequently the entire input stream should consist of 8 characters before the RETURN key (shown as [R] below) is pressed. If the first value does not have 5 digits take great care to enter leading spaces; likewise for the second value. Failure to adhere strictly to this will cause unpredictable results. I use the caret (^) symbol to denote spaces.

```
      PROGRAM IOFRMT
 10   READ (*,32) KK,LL
 32   FORMAT (I5,I3)
      PRINT *, KK,LL
      GOTO 10
      END

run

? 23^34[R]
  ^2334    0   ..... 1st entry is wrong
? ^^^23^34[R]
  ^^^23^^^^34  ..... 2nd entry correct
? ^23^127[R]
  ^^^231^27    ..... 3rd entry is wrong
```

Figure 9.4

Note that in the first example both numbers were placed within the first field width of 5. KK takes on the value 2334, LL the value of 0. In the third example, 127 was placed within the field width of 5. The digit 1 becomes part of KK, leaving 27 for LL.

Not all computers will necessarily perform as the CDC CYBER system did in the above. You may wish to see exactly how your computer works by using the above program, IOFRMT.

There seems to be little advantage in using FORMAT statements when data has to be typed in via a keyboard. It is much more convenient to employ free-format and merely type in values separated by commas. This avoids having to worry about spaces and field widths. However, if someone else has created a data file and stored it on a disc, then you may have to use FORMAT statements. An example of this is given in Chapter 14, Figure 14.14, after a discussion about record structure, and further numeric types and edit descriptors.

READing REAL numbers

The Fw.d is used for READing real values and is used in the same way as for WRITE statements. To read the following input stream from a data file or keyboard entry:

123.4^^86.5^^5.23456

I would need a FORMAT statement as shown:

```
      READ (*,35) A1,A2,A3
 35   FORMAT (F5.1, 2X, F4.1, 2X, F7.5)

or: 35   FORMAT (F5.1,F6.1,F9.5)
```

Figure 9.5

In the second case, I include the spaces within the Fw. Note the absence of commas in the input stream.

To read the following input stream: 12345^^34.56^^^45.009^^^^987 I would need:

```
either:
      READ (*,40) I,A,B,J
 40   FORMAT (I5,2X,F5.2,2X,F6.3,4X,I3)

or: 40   FORMAT (I5,F7.2,F8.3,I7)
```

Figure 9.6

I think you may now agree that using free FORMAT for the following data values is much simpler than using a FORMAT statement:

?12345,34.56,45.009,987[Return]

Further points

1. If a comment is placed on the same line as the WRITE statement rather than within the FORMAT, the A descriptor (for alphanumeric type) is required, thus:

```
      WRITE (*,56) 'HERE IS A COMMENT'
 56   FORMAT (10X, A)
```

The A also has a w field and specifies the number of characters, including spaces, within the single quotes. If the w-idth field is omitted, as above, the computer will supply the number on our behalf.

2. Another symbol which can be included in a FORMAT statement is the / (solidus or backslash). This will cause the printer mechanism (or screen software) to move to the next line before printing or displaying whatever follows, thus:

```
      WRITE (*,60) A,B,C
60    FORMAT (F6.3,//,F6.3,//F6.3)
```

This will cause values A, B and C to appear on separate lines separated by a blank line.

3. Each time a READ or WRITE statement is executed, the computer moves to the next record (READ) or next print line (WRITE). This has undesirable effects in certain situations. In Chapter 14 we discuss this in relation to the implied DO-loop.

4. We may use repetition factors within FORMAT.

```
      WRITE (*,70) JJ, LL, KK
70    FORMAT (I5,2X,I5,2X,I5)  or  (3(I5,2X))
```

Since I5,2X is required three times, a repetition factor can be placed as shown. It simply means to repeat what is in parentheses three times. Note well the correct number of opening and closing parentheses!

5. The maximum value that the w may take will frequently depend on the computer system being used. In the case of large mainframe computers devoted to number crunching this may be as large as 15 or more. If the value exceeds the maximum w-idth supported, it will be displayed in exponent form; see Chapter 14.

6. Do make sure that you do not confuse a variable with an integer edit descriptor. I3 in the following WRITE statement is a variable; the I3 in the FORMAT is an edit descriptor:

```
      WRITE (*,80) I3
80    FORMAT (I3)
```

7. PRINT may also have a FORMAT statement. The above would become:

```
      PRINT 80, I3
80    FORMAT (I3)
```

8. If you would like leading zeros to be output rather than blanks, the Iw can be extended to Iw.m where the m stands for the number of positions in which leading zeros may appear. Thus:

```
      WRITE (*,90) JJ              WRITE (*,90) JJ
90    FORMAT (I7.5)         90    FORMAT (I7.7)

      ^^00123                     0000123
```

If JJ contained 123, the first m (5) would produce two leading zeros; the second m (7) would produce four. The m-field, of course, should not exceed the w-field.

9. Placing an array name in a PRINT or WRITE statement will result in the entire array being printed out. In free-format, the computer will print as many values on one line as it can. In formatted output, the FORMAT statement will control the number of values to be printed out on one line.

```
        DIMENSION N(6)          1   2   3   4   5
        . . . . . . . . . . . . . . .       6
        PRINT *, N
        PRINT 50, N             1   2   3
   50   FORMAT (3(I3,2X))        4   5   6
```

Figure 9.7

Exercises

1. Explain the function of I5 in each line of the following code:

```
        READ (*,32) I5
   32   FORMAT (I5)
```

2. Code the relevant output statements to display the following:

a) Write out three column headings (e.g. HEADING A, HEADING B) each separated by 10 spaces with the first heading indented by 5 spaces.

b) Output 3 real values on the same line, rounded to 3 decimal places and within a field width of 10. The first value should be indented by 7 spaces. Each value should be separated by 3 spaces.

3. a) For the input stream given below, what digits will the variables contain according to the READ–FORMAT statement?

```
        READ (*,100) II,JJ,KK
  100   FORMAT (I3,3X,I5,1X,I2)
        READ (*,100) LL,MM

             ? 1234567890111213[Return]
```

Figure 9.8

b) What will be read into LL and MM?

4. Where do comments to annotate output results have to be placed in WRITE formatted statements?

5. *Program Exercise 9.1: Amend Program Exercise 8.2 to include FORMAT statements which will produce the following output.

```
VALUES   READ IN
     nnn.nn
     nnn.nn etc.
TOTAL   = xxxx.xx
AVERAGE =  yy.yy
NUMBERS LESS THAN AVERAGE
     nn.nn
     nn.nn etc.
```

Figure 9.9

Chapter 10 File Handling

Cycle 1

So far, any data required by a program has been entered via the keyboard and all results have been sent to the screen or printer. What we now examine is how a program may read data from a magnetic device rather than from a keyboard and to write information to a magnetic device rather than to a printer or screen. For example, data could be logged by weather stations miles out to sea in the North Atlantic and transferred to floppy discs or large mainframe rigid discs for subsequent processing. Furthermore, one program may generate results which are to be stored on disc so that another program may use those results as input data.

Data is READ or WRITten to a magnetic device via an OPEN statement and a corresponding unit number in place of the first asterisk in the READ or WRITE statement. In Figure 10.1 we see our familiar READ and WRITE statements with two asterisks placed in parentheses. The first asterisk in a READ statement informs the computer that data is to come from the keyboard or, in a WRITE statement, that information is to be sent to the screen. However, if we put a number in place of the first asterisk, this tells the computer that information is to be read from or be written to some other source.

```
READ  (*,*)  Al,B
WRITE (*,*)  Al,B

READ  (u,sl) variables
WRITE (u,sl) variables
```

Figure 10.1

where: u = unit number in range 1–99 (for large mainframes)
        sl = statement label in range 1–99999.
             (see Chapter 9, Cycle 2 for FORMAT statement)

On some computers, the range for the unit number is much less than 1–99. It would be more sensible to keep the unit number in a smaller range, say, 1–15.

Let us suppose that a series of integer values have been stored in a data file called DATFIL and that this file is held on a floppy disc. Each number has to be read one at a time from this file into an array called NUM. This is shown in Figure 10.2. Note the presence of the digit 3 (any

81

value in range 1–99 could have been chosen). This tells the computer that data is to be read from a data file rather than the input stream from the keyboard. But to what does the digit 3 refer? This is what the computer wants to know as well.

```
      PROGRAM IOFILE
      DIMENSION NUM(20)
      OPEN(3,FILE='DATFIL')
      DO 100 K=1,20
         READ (3,*) NUM(K)
 100  CONTINUE
```

Figure 10.2

OPEN statement

It is the OPEN statement which provides the link to a particular data file. Note the presence of the digit 3 after the opening parenthesis and that the data file (DATFIL) is also referred to. The 3 is the so-called unit number and links a READ (or WRITE) statement with this particular OPEN statement. After the unit number, the relevant data file is named by putting it inside single quotes after FILE =.

```
      OPEN (3, FILE = 'DATFIL')
```

When a READ (3, *) is encountered during execution, the computer 'searches' for the OPEN statement with the same unit number in order to find the name of the file being referred to. It will now OPEN that file and read the data into the array and/or variables specified in the READ statement.

A fuller version of the OPEN statement includes the word UNIT =

```
      OPEN (UNIT = 3, FILE='DATFIL')
```

but as implied, this is optional. In the program code which follows, data is being read from a data file called DATFIL as well as being written to a data file called DATA2.

```
      OPEN (UNIT = 2, FILE = 'DATFIL')
      OPEN (UNIT = 3, FILE = 'DATA2')
      DO 100 L=1,20
         READ (2,*) NUM
         X = NUM * 1.15
         WRITE (3,*) X
 100  CONTINUE
```

Figure 10.3

Here, the first number from DATFIL is read into NUM, a computation performed and the result stored in variable X. The programmer asks for the value in X to be written to UNIT 3 rather than to the screen/printer. The computer 'looks back' to the OPEN statement for one which has UNIT=3 so that it can locate the name of the data file. In our case this has been called DATA2.

Nothing will appear on the screen unless we include a second WRITE statement:

```
WRITE (*,*) X
```

Now the value in X will be displayed onto the screen as well as being sent to the magnetic device to be stored in a file called DATA2.

Before execution DATA2 does not exist. However, during execution, the computer system will create this new file automatically and store the results under the name DATA2.

More about OPEN

1. The OPEN statement provides the compiler with certain information. It is a common practice to place this statement at the start of the program.

2. It is possible to WRITE to a file in one part of a program and, in another part, to REWIND a file back to the beginning for subsequent READing.

```
         PROGRAM BIGTOT
         DIMENSION TOTALS(10)
         OPEN (4, FILE = 'DATA3')
         TOT = 0.0
C
C     1st Loop: write TOTs to unit 4
C
         DO 200 K = 1,10
            READ (*,*) NUM1,NUM2,NUM3
            TOT = NUM1+NUM2+NUM3
            WRITE (4,*) 'TOTAL = ',TOT
200      CONTINUE
C
C     2nd Loop: rewind unit 4 and read back TOTs
C
         REWIND(4)
         GRNTOT = 0.0
         DO 300 L = 1,10
            READ (4,*) TOTALS(L)
            GRNTOT = GRNTOT+TOTALS(L)
300   CONTINUE
         WRITE (*,*) 'GRAND TOTAL = ', GRNTOT
         STOP
         END
```

Figure 10.4

The first DO-loop reads in three values from the keyboard, totals them up and writes the total to DATA3. This is repeated 10 times so that DATA3 has ten sets of totals. The data file is then rewound to the beginning. The second DO-loop reads in the ten sets of TOTs into an array and computes the grand total.

If the REWIND statement were omitted, the READ (4, *) statement would try to read a value from the end of DATA3. The effect would be to read past the end-of-file and the program would abort.

REWIND (u)

The REWIND statement will simply rewind to the beginning a file which has been associated with the unit number specified within parentheses. The file name must not be given. If the file is already at the beginning, no action is taken (and no harm done!).

> *Tip*: When using OPEN statements, it is always advisable to REWIND the files before any processing takes place. This avoids complications when a program has to be corrected and re-run.
>
> Each time a program reads a value from or writes a value to a file, the computer moves a pointer to the next value. It is by this pointer that the computer keeps track of its position within a file. Should a program contain a run-time error, the normal thing to do is to correct the error and re-execute the program. But where is the pointer? It may not be at the beginning. To ensure that at each execution of the program, the pointers are at the start of the files, take the precaution of inserting REWIND statements (one for each file) before any other executable statement.

CLOSE statement

The CLOSE statement tells the computer to disconnect a file from a unit number. That unit number may then become associated with some other file at the programmer's discretion. The form of the statement is:

```
CLOSE (2, STATUS = 'KEEP')
```

It is the unit number (2 above) which specifies the file to be closed. We do not use the file name itself. If the status is set to 'KEEP', as above, the file will remain in existence after execution of the CLOSE statement. It is then up to the user to save the file permanently once the program terminates. Otherwise, if the computer is switched off before this done the file will not be saved for future use.

If the status is set to 'DELETE' the file associated with the specified unit number ceases to exist and the space it took up in memory is now freed.

If the CLOSE statement is not used within the program, then the file associated with the unit number will automatically be given the status 'KEEP'.

The following statements have the same effect:

```
CLOSE (2)        CLOSE (UNIT =2, STATUS = 'KEEP')
```

Note that UNIT = is optional.

System file names

If a digit exists in place of the first asterisk in READ and WRITE statements, then there has got to be a corresponding OPEN statement even if the data is to be typed at the keyboard or results sent to the printer. So, what file names are we going to give to the keyboard and printer/screen?

Each computer installation will have chosen them for us. In the example below, INPUT happens to be the system name for the keyboard, OUTPUT for the screen/printer. In other installations STANIN (standard input device) is used for the keyboard, STANOUT for the screen/printer. Others again invent something else. You will need to find out!

```
OPEN  (5, FILE = 'INPUT')
OPEN  (6, FILE = 'OUTPUT')
READ  (5,*) NUM
WRITE (6,*) NUM
```

Figure 10.5

When the above READ statement is executed, the computer 'searches for' the file name in the relevant OPEN statement associated with UNIT = 5. On finding the name 'INPUT' it will display the input prompt onto the screen so that data can be entered at the keyboard. The WRITE statement specifies unit 6. Since this is associated with the FILE = 'OUTPUT', the results will be sent to the screen or printer.

> Some early Fortran IV programs always used digit 5 for input and 6 for output rather than using asterisks. If you have to make use of such a program, you could go through the program changing the digits back to asterisks but in a long program you might miss some and this would generate compilation errors. It may be much quicker to insert the two OPEN statements and be certain that all READs and WRITEs with those digits will execute properly.

In Figure 10.3, it is assumed that the data file (DATFIL) has exactly 20 integer values. Suppose it is not known how many values a file contains: let us say that they could range from 1 to 50. We would have to set the DO-loop counter to 50 but how would we know when the end-of-file is reached?

Let us assume that on a given occasion, DATFIL contains 31 values. The 32nd 'position' is the end-of-file marker (EOF) (see Figure 10.6). Along with the 31 data values (records), there are two additional 'records' which are used to mark the beginning of the data file (BOI, beginning of information) and the end of the file (EOF). These marker records are used by the computer system when it transfers files to or from central memory.

Since the DO-loop is set to repeat 50 times, on the 32nd READ, it will encounter the EOF marker. This will immediately cause the program to abort! The system does this to warn us that there are no more data values to read in. Although this is very kind, it is not very practical.

BOI	value 1	value 2	.....	value 30	value 31	EOF

     DATFIL

Figure 10.6

However, there is a way to prevent the run-time system from taking such drastic steps every time it meets an EOF marker. We can add 'END=nnn' to our READ statement, as seen in Figure 10.7, where 'nnn' is a statement label. What this is saying is that during the reading of a data file, if EOF is encountered, do not abort the program, I know what I am doing, please move to the statement label 30 (in our case).

```
        OPEN (UNIT = 2, FILE = 'DATFIL')
        OPEN (UNIT = 3, FILE = 'DATA2')
        REWIND(2)
        REWIND(3)
        KOUNT = 0
        DO 100 L=1,20
            READ (2,*,END=30) NUM
            KOUNT = KOUNT+1
            X = NUM * 1.15
            WRITE (3,*) X
100     CONTINUE
30      next instruction … .
```

Figure 10.7

The final point to discuss is how can we tell the actual number of values read in? This can be done quite simply by inserting a counter *after* the READ statement:

```
        KOUNT = KOUNT+1
```

Note that it must come after the READ so that we do not count the occurrence of reading the EOF marker, thus making the counter 32 instead of 31.

> Note that PRINT *, and READ *, make no provision for file handling, unlike READ (*, *) and WRITE (*, *). The single asterisk in the first two statements may refer only to FORMAT statements.

Exercises: Cycle 1

1. *Program Exercise 10.1: Write a program which will create a small data file containing about 10 real numbers. (You may like to generate the numbers via the random number generator on your system. Rewind the file, read data from this data file, calculate the sum and average of the numbers and print out the results.

2. If you forget to put in a CLOSE statement, what will happen?

3. What is achieved by the following and why could it be useful?

```
CLOSE (UNIT=3, STATUS='DELETE')
```

Cycle 2

OPEN and CLOSE

OPEN (openlist items)

where openlist items are:

UNIT = u
FILE = name
STATUS = stat
ACCESS = acc
FORM = fm
RECL = rl
BLANK = blnk
ERR = s
IOSTAT = ios

The openlist may include any of the above separated by commas. Items may be written in any order and UNIT = may be ommitted. If so, the unit number must be the first item.

u	is the unit number as previously defined (Cycle 1).
name	is a character expression denoting the name of the file as discussed in Cycle 1.
stat	is a character expression with value 'OLD', 'NEW'. 'SCRATCH' or UNKNOWN'.
	if 'OLD', the file must already exist.
	if 'NEW' the file must not exist and will be created.
	if 'SCRATCH' an unnamed file will be connected for use during the life of the pro-program and will be deleted upon terminationof the program.
	if 'UNKNOWN' the status of the file will depend upon the defaults of a particular installation.
acc	is a character expression with the value 'SEQUENTIAL' if the file to be connected is a sequential file (see Glossary), or 'DIRECT' if the file to be connected is a direct access file. If the item is omitted, a sequential file is assumed.

fm   is a character expression with the value 'FORMATTED' if the file is to be accessed
           via formatted statements, or, 'UNFORMATTED' if the file is to be accessed with
           unformatted input statements. If it is omitted, formatted files are assumed for
           sequential access files, unformatted is assumed for direct access files.

rl   is a positive integer value defining the length of records for direct access files. The
           length refers to the number of characters (including spaces) in each record. This
           item must be included for direct access files, otherwise it must be left out.

blnk   is a character expression with the value 'NULL' if all blanks in numeric fields are to
           be ignored. However, if a field contains all blanks, then zero is assumed. If this item
           contains the value 'ZERO', then blanks are treated as zeros. If the item is omitted,
           'NULL' is assumed. It can only be used with formatted files.

s and ios are defined in the READ and WRITE section above.

Examples

```
OPEN(10, FILE = 'XYZ', STATUS = 'NEW')
```

This opens a file on unit 10 with the name XYZ. The file must not already exist since it will be
created during execution. By default it will be a sequential file containing formatted records
and any blanks in numeric field will be ignored. It must be read from and written to using
formatted read and write statements.

```
OPEN(2, STATUS = 'SCRATCH', ACCESS = 'DIRECT', RECL = 40,
FORM = 'FORMATTED', BLANK = 'ZERO', IOSTAT = IOS, ERR =
300)
```

This will open an unnamed, scratch file on unit 2. It will contain formatted records all with
length 40 characters. Blanks in the numeric fields of the record will be treated as zeros. Any
error on opening the file will cause statement 300 to be executed and IOS will be given a value
which can be tested within the program. Since it is a scratch file, it can be used as a temporary
work space which will be deleted upon termination of the program.

CLOSE (closelist items)

The items for use with the CLOSE statement are:

UNIT = u
IOSTST = IOS
ERR = s
STATUS = stat

u, ios and s have been defined previously.

stat   is a character expression which may take one of the following values: 'KEEP',
           'DELETE'. These were defined earlier in Cycle 1. But note that if the file was
           opened as a scratch file, then it cannot be closed as a 'KEEP' file.

Chapter 11   Subroutines

Cycle 1

Professional programmers write very short programs involving as few as twenty instructions, in some instances. Yet 'serious' programs consist of hundreds, even thousands of instructions. So, we have a dilemma! How to write short yet long programs.

Modular programming

Any major or complex task may always be broken down into a series of smaller sub-tasks or modules. For example, engineers working on a motorway project must plan in advance and divide the overall project into an organised and related set of sub-tasks. No one would begin the motorway at point A and simply push it forward until point B is reached hoping to overcome problems as and when they arise. This would be hopelessly inefficient.

The same applies to any major programming task. It has to be planned in advance and broken down into sub-tasks. This is illustrated in Figure 11.1. The payroll program is not one task but several inter-related tasks. At the very least it can be sub-divided into three major units – input of data, processing of data, output of results.

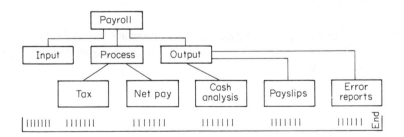

Figure 11.1

If one of these modules is complex, it too can be further subdivided into smaller and more manageable sub-tasks. For example, one aspect of the processing of an employee's data is to calculate the tax. Here is a sub-task which is more convenient to handle separately.

After the individual modules have been written, they are linked together into one total program.

Subroutines

In Fortran, modular programming is achieved by the use of subroutines. A subroutine is a group of instructions, headed by the SUBROUTINE statement and designed to perform a given sub-task. Figure 11.2 shows the structure of a typical Fortran program.

Note that each subroutine has its own END statement, including the main routine. This is because the Fortran compiler translates each subroutine as a separate 'program' or *sub-program*. The END statement tells the compiler that this routine has no more statements. We shall soon see that this has a rather serious implication.

Creating a subroutine

A subroutine is created by using the keyword SUBROUTINE (column 7 onwards) and by giving the routine a unique name. This name may be up to six characters as with variable names. However, there is *no type* implication in the choice of name, i.e. one is not restricted to doing only integer 'things' or only real 'things'. Within the same subroutine, integer, real and character processing may take place.

Execution of a subroutine

In a program which contains one or more subroutines there must be a *main routine* containing the PROGRAM statement. The subroutines follow the main routine and may be in any order. It is the purpose of the main routine to activate the instructions in subroutines and in the order required. This is done via a CALL statement.

The CALLing statement

In Figure 11.2 we see a program consisting of a main routine and two subroutines. At some point in the main routine, it becomes necessary to execute those instructions in SUB1. The CALL SUB1 statement does this.

```
Main        PROGRAM SUBS
Routine     ............
            ............
            CALL SUB1
            ............
            CALL SUB2
            CALL SUB1
            ............
            ............
            END
```

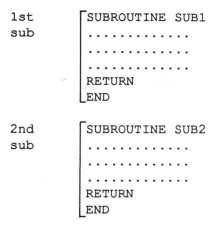

```
1st        SUBROUTINE SUB1
sub        . . . . . . . . . . . .
           . . . . . . . . . . . .
           . . . . . . . . . . . .
           RETURN
           END


2nd        SUBROUTINE SUB2
sub        . . . . . . . . . . . .
           . . . . . . . . . . . .
           . . . . . . . . . . . .
           RETURN
           END
```

Figure 11.2

When the CALL SUB1 instruction is encountered in the main program, this has the effect of telling the computer to pass control of execution to the subroutine named SUB1 and to begin execution of instructions from that point. When all the instructions have been executed in SUB1, it is the RETURN statement that forces the computer to resume execution at the instruction *after* the CALLing statement in the main routine.

When the CALL SUB2 statement is executed, the computer begins execution of instructions within that routine until the RETURN statement is encountered. The computer then returns to the next instruction after the CALL SUB2. In the example above, this is another CALL to SUB1. So, routine SUB1 is re-executed. In this way, one routine may be executed time and again.

We may now begin to appreciate the importance of the main routine. It states the order in which subroutines are to be executed and the number of times they need to be executed. In consequence, there is no importance attached to the physical placing of subroutines within a program but it does matter where the CALL statements are placed in the main routine.

An example

We can use the temperature conversion program to illustrate the use of subroutines.

```
     PROGRAM TMPCF3
     DO 100 L = 1,10
         READ (*,*) TEMP, ITYPE
         IF (ITYPE .EQ. 1) THEN
             CALL CELCON
         ELSE
             CALL FAHCON
         ENDIF
100  CONTINUE
     END
```

```
      SUBROUTINE CELCON
C
C convert to Celsius
C
      C = (5.0/9.0)*(TEMP-32)
      WRITE (*,*) 'CELSIUS = ',C,'FAHRENHEIT = ',TEMP
      RETURN
      END


      SUBROUTINE FAHCON
C
C convert to Fahrenheit
C
      F = (9.0/5.0)*TEMP + 32
      WRITE (*,*) 'FAHRENHEIT = ',F, 'CELSIUS = ',TEMP
      RETURN
      END
```

Figure 11.3

Explanation of TMPCF3

If the program discovers that the type read in is 1 (i.e. a Fahrenheit temperature), a CALL is made to SUBROUTINE CELCON. The computer begins to execute the instructions in CELCON until it meets the RETURN statement. At this point, the computer is forced back to the main routine and to the instruction after CALL CELCON. Since this is the ELSE statement, the computer 'moves down' to the instruction after the ENDIF which is the end-of-loop instruction. The DO-loop is then repeated.

When a type 2 is read in, the computer is forced to execute instructions in SUBROUTINE FAHCON until it meets the RETURN statement. This will force the computer to return to the ENDIF statement, which in turn will force the computer to execute the end-of-loop instruction.

However, there is one little problem. The program will not work! This is because each subroutine is compiled as a separate program entity. We shall now discuss why the program will not work and then see how to overcome the problem.

The effect of individual compilation of subroutines

The compiler treats each subroutine and the main routine as separate programs, hence the need for the END statement in each one. This has a useful side-effect but causes a problem.

Each routine (including the main routine) is given its own *local* data area in central memory as shown in Figure 11.4. Variable names and statement numbers are therefore local to that routine. In Figure 11.4, we see that both the variable K and the statement number 23 occur in each routine but there will be no confusion.

```
SUBROUTINE ONE                        SUBROUTINE TWO
. . . . . . . . . . . .                . . . . . . . . . . . . . .
23  K = K+1           K[   ]    23    K = K+3            K[   ]
. . . . . . . . . . . .                . . . . . . . . . . . . . .
. . . . . . . . . . . .                GOTO 23
RETURN                                RETURN
END                                   END
```

Figure 11.4

The GOTO statement in SUBROUTINE TWO will go to its own local label 23 and not to the statement 23 in SUBROUTINE ONE. Likewise, when 3 is added to the variable K, it will be its local K and not that of SUBROUTINE ONE. The advantage of this is that, if someone else has written a routine which we would like to use, we can insert the routine as a SUBROUTINE in our own program. But we do not have to worry about whether the rest of our program uses the same variable names or statement labels!

However, it does mean that if we *do want* a variable in one routine to be the same variable in another, then we have a problem. Let us illustrate this by the following.

I need to read in a number via one subroutine and to output that same number via another as in Figure 11.5.

```
PROGRAM INOUT1
CALL IN
CALL OUT
STOP
END
- - - - - - - - - - - - - - - - - - - - -
SUBROUTINE IN
READ (*,*) X           X[    12.6]
RETURN
END
- - - - - - - - - - - - - - - - - - - - -
SUBROUTINE OUT
WRITE (*,*) X
RETURN                 X[      ?]
END
```

Figure 11.5

Although we would not dream of constructing subroutines for such a trivial task, it will illustrate the problem. The main routine is executed and the first executable instruction is a CALL to SUBROUTINE IN. This routine reads in the value 12.6 into its local data area and stores it in variable X. The RETURN forces control back to the next instruction in the main routine. This is a CALL to SUBROUTINE OUT. Here, we ask for the contents of X (which is local to this routine) to be written out. But because X is local it is not the same as X in routine IN. So we are not sure what will be printed out.

What we need to be able to do is to tell the compiler that X in both routines must refer to the same location. There are two methods of doing this, by *arguments* and by the COMMON statement. We shall discuss the first now, and leave the COMMON to Cycle 2.

Solving the problem by arguments

A subroutine may be given one or more arguments, sometimes also called *parameters*. These are ordinary variables and are attached to the subroutine name in both the CALL and the SUBROUTINE statements. Let us suppose that a given routine (PRINT) has to print out the value in a variable called A which has been computed in the main routine (see Figure 11.6).

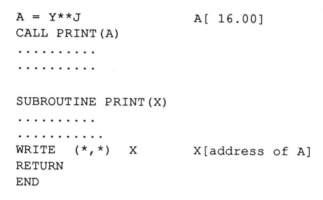

```
A = Y**J                A[ 16.00]
CALL PRINT(A)
..........
..........


SUBROUTINE PRINT(X)
..........
..........
WRITE   (*,*)   X        X[address of A]
RETURN
END
```

Figure 11.6

The CALL to the PRINT routine has the variable name A enclosed in parentheses. This is the argument. We are saying that routine PRINT must be executed and that the value in variable A is going to be used. In the SUBROUTINE PRINT we also have an argument called X and this too is enclosed in parentheses. Within this routine we ask for the value in the argument X to be written out.

This next paragraph is important. The argument in the CALL statement is called the *actual argument*. It contains the name of the variable which we actually want to use. The argument in the subroutine name is called a *dummy argument*. It purpose is to hold the *address* of the actual argument.

This is how it works. During run-time, the CALL PRINT(A) is executed. Control now passes to routine PRINT, and the dummy argument X is given the address of the actual argument, A. Any reference to X now becomes a direct reference to variable A.

Consequently, when the WRITE (*,*) X instruction is executed, the computer remembers that X is a dummy argument and merely 'looks in' location X to find the address of the location (variable A) which it really has to WRITE out.

Why not call the dummy argument A and avoid any confusion? That is a question frequently asked by the beginner. There is no reason why you cannot call it A. But do you remember that we said that subroutines can be re-executed many times within the same program? Now look at Figure 11.7. The main routine continues with its execution until it asks for the PRINT routine to be executed again. But this time, the program wants the routine to write out the value stored in the location called B. Where would we be if the dummy argument had been called A? We would now have to remember that any reference to dummy A is really a reference to the actual argument B.

It is important that you make clear this distinction between the actual argument in the CALL statement and the dummy in the routine. The dummy is not so much a variable name as a location to hold the address (during run-time) of an actual argument. Consequently, many Fortran programmers invent different names for dummy arguments to emphasise this distinction.

```
A = Y**J                 A[ 16.00]
CALL PRINT(A)

. . . . . . . . . .
B = A**3
CALL PRINT(B)            B[5096.00]

. . . . . . . . . .


SUBROUTINE PRINT(X)

. . . . . . . . . .
. . . . . . . . . .
WRITE (*,*) X            X[address of B]
RETURN
END
```

Figure 11.7

During execution of the CALL PRINT (B) , the address of location B is passed over to the dummy argument X. Any reference to X within this routine is now a direct reference to location B.

Let us return to the problem in PROGRAM INOUT1 (Figure 11.5). Figure 11.8 shows the solution. The CALL IN has an argument A. During execution, routine IN will contain the address of location A in its dummy argument X. The READ (*, *) X will consequently cause the value 12.6 to be placed in location A. The CALL to OUT has the argument A and during execution, the dummy argument of routine OUT (X) will be given the address of location A. Thus, when

```
WRITE (*,*) X
```

is executed, it will be the value in location A which will be written out.

```
PROGRAM INOUT2
CALL IN(A)               A[    12.6]
CALL OUT(A)
```

```
      STOP
      END

      SUBROUTINE IN(X)
      READ (*,*) X              X[address of A]
      RETURN
      END

      SUBROUTINE OUT(X)
      WRITE (*,*) X
      RETURN                    X[address of A]
      END
```

Figure 11.8

Program TMPCF4

We can now return to the program which did not work and attach arguments to the relevant instructions. It will now work because the address of variable TEMP has been passed over to routines FAHCON and CELCON as an argument.

```
      PROGRAM TMPCF4
      DO 100 L = 1,10
         READ (*,*) TEMP, ITYPE
         IF (ITYPE .EQ. 1) THEN
            CALL CELCON(TEMP)
         ELSE
            CALL FAHCON(TEMP)
         ENDIF
 100  CONTINUE
      END

      SUBROUTINE CELCON(XTEMP)
C
C     convert to Celsius
C
      C = (5.0/9.0)*(XTEMP-32)
      WRITE (*,*) 'CELSIUS = ',C,'FAHRENHEIT = ',XTEMP
      RETURN
      END

      SUBROUTINE FAHCON(XTEMP)
C
C     convert to Fahrenheit
C
      F = (9.0/5.0)*XTEMP + 32
      WRITE (*,*) 'FAHRENHEIT = ',F,'CELSIUS = ',XTEMP
      RETURN
      END
```

Figure 11.9

Note

If a CALL statement has an argument, the subroutine must also have an argument! We discuss arguments in more detail in Cycle 2 and also examine the second method of communicating variables across subroutines using COMMON.

Exercises: Cycle 1

1. Explain why modular programming is a useful technique to adopt.

2. How is modular programming achieved in Fortran?

3. Explain the purpose for the RETURN and END in subroutines.

4. What is the implication of both the main routine and subroutines being compiled separately?

5. What are dummy and actual arguments?

6. *Program Exercise 11.1: Amend the program TMPCF4 so that the program will stop execution at the user's request and, also, trap as invalid any type entered which is not 1 or 2.

Cycle 2

Order, type and number

More than one argument can be used in the CALLing statement, each separated by a comma, thus:

```
CALL NAME3(X,Y,I)
..........
SUBROUTINE NAME3(XX,YY,II)
```

However, the order, the type and the number of arguments in both the CALL and SUBROUTINE statements must be identical! The first argument in the CALL statement will be matched with the first dummy argument of the SUBROUTINE, the second with the the second, and so forth. If there is any type mismatch, errors could occur. If the number of arguments differ in either list, the compiler (at least some compilers) will not execute the program.

Passing and returning values

Values may be passed by the CALL statement to a subroutine; the subroutine may pass back values to the CALLing program unit. Look at Figure 11.10.

```
M = 2*5                    M[   10]
CALL SUBX(M,N)             N[   50]
K = N*3                    K[  150]
WRITE (*,*) K

SUBROUTINE SUBX(I,J)
J = I*5                    I[address of M]
RETURN                     J[address of N]
END
```

Figure 11.10

I is given the address of M; J is given the address of N. Variable M passes the value 10 to the dummy argument I in SUBX. SUBX computes the value 50 using I (i.e. value in M) and passes the result to dummy J which puts the result in location N. Thus, on RETURN, N has the value 50.

There is no reason why one argument cannot do both tasks. The following program segment achieves the same as the one in Figure 11.10, except that the argument M does both tasks.

```
M = 2*5
CALL SUBX(M)
K = M*3
WRITE (*,*) K

SUBROUTINE SUBX(I)
I = I*5
RETURN
END
```

Figure 11.11

Personally, I prefer the version in Figure 11.10. It is quite clear what is happening and there can be no confusion. In the second case, where the one argument is performing two tasks, there is a danger that someone (even the originator of the program) will confuse the function it is performing at any one time.

Types of arguments

Arguments may be:

- simple variables
- subscripted variables
- dimensioned arrays.

In Figure 11.12, we see that the main routine has two one- dimensional arrays, X and K. The entire array X is passed over to SUBROUTINE SUBXK, but just the fifth element of array K.

```
PROGRAM XXX
DIMENSION X(100), K(50)
........
CALL SUBXK(X,K(5),RES)
WRITE (*,*) RES
........
END

SUBROUTINE SUBXK(XX,K5,R)
DIMENSION XX(100)
.........
R = computation
RETURN
END
```

Figure 11.12

Note that in Fortran, it is necessary to create a *dummy dimension* for the array XX. Failure to do so will cause the compiler to complain and prevent execution. We can think of the dummy dimension as being a single location with the starting address of the actual array X. In other words, it does not allocate a second set of 100 locations for XX.

Note also that the name of the array is all that is required in the CALL statement. Since it has been declared as an array in the DIMENSION statement, X cannot be a single variable.

In the case of K(5) in the CALLing statement, we pass over the fifth element of array K. However, we need only a single variable name in the subroutine's argument list, K5 above.

COMMON **statement**

The second method of passing variables between program units is via the COMMON statement. After the keyword COMMON, we list all those variables which we would like to be common to other routines. The compiler will reserve a common area of memory and place all the variables there. A reference to any of the variables in this common area may be made by any routine.

```
COMMON A,B,C,D,I,J,K
```

But there are conditions! We can discuss these in relation to the following, Figure 11.13:

```
PROGRAM CMMON                      COMMON
DIMENSION A(3)            A(1) [          ] 1
COMMON A,B,C,I,J,X        A(2) [          ] 2
........                  A(3) [          ] 3
........                    B [          ] 4
CALL ONE                    C [          ] 5
```

```
WRITE (*,*) X                    X[          ] 6
........
CALL TWO
WRITE (*,*) X
END

SUBROUTINE ONE
COMMON A,B,C,I,J,X
X = B*C
RETURN
END

SUBROUTINE TWO                   LOCAL
X = B*C                     B[          ]
RETURN                      C[          ]
END                         X[          ]
```

Figure 11.13

When a COMMON variable is required in a routine, that routine *must* contain a COMMON statement, otherwise the variables will be local to the routine. Thus, since SUBROUTINE TWO does not have a COMMON statement, variables X, B and C are local to TWO. (Note that neither B nor C have been given values and that the program will probably abort at that point!) However, in the case of SUBROUTINE ONE, since it does have the COMMON statement, X, B and C will refer directly to those variables in the COMMON area (also called COMMON block). Thus, on return from ONE, the value in COMMON X will be written out.

But why do I put *all* the variables in the COMMON statement of SUBROUTINE TWO? Why not simply write: COMMON B, C, X ? Here is one of the reasons why the use of COMMON can lead to errors.

The main trouble is that human beings view matters differently to the computer. We see *names* in the COMMON statement, the computer sees *positions*. Every time the computer comes across a COMMON statement, the first variable is associated with the first location in the common block; the second variable with the second location; etc. It does not try to match names of variables. Thus, if I had put the following:

```
COMMON B,C,X
```

in SUBROUTINE ONE, then B will refer to the first location in COMMON, namely, A(1). C will be associated with the second location [A(2)]; X with the third location, [A(3)].

It is permissible to dimension an array in the COMMON statement. The two following segments of code achieve the same, but note that if we use both the DIMENSION and COMMON statements, the DIMENSION must come first.

```
DIMENSION A(50)        COMMON A(50), B,C
COMMON A, B, C
```

The full form

```
COMMON/blockname/list of variables
```

An optional name can be given to the entire common block:

```
COMMON /BLK1/A(50),B,C
```

Furthermore, we may have more than one block name:

```
COMMON /BLK1/A(50),B,C,/BLK2/I,J,K
```

The comma between the two blocks is optional. Having 'created' two blocks, I need to refer only to that block which is relevant in a given subroutine.

```
COMMON/BLK1/A(3),I,J /BLK2/B,C,X
CALL ONE
.........
SUBROUTINE ONE
COMMON/BLK2/B,C,X
X = B*C
PRINT *, X
RETURN
END
```

Figure 11.14

Programs with vast amounts of data which cannot fit into memory at one time can take advantage of the fact that Fortran allows different variable names to be allocated to the same common location. However, great care is required by the programmer to ensure that the correct data is sitting in the correct location at the right time. It is *not* a practice to recommend. The EQUIVALENCE statement does the same, but it should be used only by experienced and careful programmers.

Arguments or COMMON?

Arguments are preferred when there are few variable names involved, otherwise it becomes all too easy to miss one out or put them in the wrong order when typing them. COMMON is frequently used when there are many variable names. To avoid incorrect typing, the secret is to type the list of names once and then use the computer's text-processing facility to copy the statement at all relevant points in the program.

Exercises: Cycle 2

1. Write a program to generate, 50 random integer numbers in the range 1–30 and possibly

including 1 and 30. Calculate the sum of the numbers; calculate the sum of their squares; and calculate the standard deviation from the following formula (or one of your own!). Create a subroutine to calculate the standard deviation. See Additional Exercise 6 in Appendix C.

$$\text{standard deviation} = \sqrt{\frac{\sum_{i=1}^{n}(X_i - \overline{X})^2}{N}}$$

$$\text{where } \overline{X} = \text{mean} = \frac{\sum X_i}{N}$$

Chapter 12   Functions–Intrinsic, Statement and Sub-Program

Cycle 2

A Fortran program must consist of a main program (main routine) and may include any number of sub-programs. These sub-programs may be called from the main routine or from any other sub-program to perform a particular task. There are four types of sub-programs:

- instrinsic functions
- statement functions
- sub-program functions
- subroutines.

We have already discussed subroutines in the previous chapter; let us now turn our attention to the functions.

Intrinsic functions

The five basic functions of arithmetic ($+ - * / **$) are not the only operations which we can perform on numbers. There are hundreds of other possibilities including logarithms, trigonometric functions, maxima and minima. These and many more are commonly available to the Fortran programmer. However, instead of being denoted by special symbols (as in the case of the five basic operations), they are referred to by names, e.g. MAX, LOG, SIN, COS, SQRT. The numbers these functions work on are placed within parentheses and are known as the arguments or *operands* of the function.

> The term *argument* means the input to a computation. An archaic meaning of the word 'argument' was related to the word 'refashioning'. The argument of SQRT(7.5) is refashioned into the value: 2.738612787526.

to discover the largest of a series of numbers, we write:

```
LARGE = MAX(1,2,3)
PRINT *, LARGE
```

Table 12.1
Arithmetic intrinsic functions

Function	Value computed	Type of result
ABS (a)	absolute value $\mid a \mid$	same as a
MAX$(a_1, a_2, ...)$	largest of two or more arguments	same as a_1, a_2,...
MIN$(a_1, a_2, ...)$	smallest of two or more arguments	same as a_1, a_2,...
MOD (a_1, a_2)	remainder of division $a_1 - $ INT$(a_1/a_2)^*a_2$	same as a_1 and a_2
SIGN(a_1, a_2)	transfer of sign; $\mid a_1 \mid$ if $a_2 \geq 0$ $- \mid a_1 \mid$ if $a_2 < 0$	same as a_1 and a_2
NINT(a)	nearest integer to a (standard rounding)	INTEGER
INT(a)	conversion to INTEGER (fraction as dropped, not rounded)	INTEGER
REAL(a)	conversion to REAL	REAL

Note: Arguments may be any type of numbers, but all the arguments in one function reference must be of the same type.

Mathematical intrinsic functions

Function	Value computed	Comments
SQRT(a)	$\sqrt{a}$	$a \geq 0$
EXP(a)	e^{a}	$e = 2.182818204590 ...$ $= $ base of natural logarithms
LOG(a)	natural logarithm	$a > 0$
LOG10(a)	base 10 logarithm	$a > 0$
SIN(a)	trigonometric sine	argument in radians
COS(a)	trigonometric cosine	argument in radians
TAN(a)	trigonometric tangent	argument in radians
ASIN(a)	arcsine	$-\dfrac{\pi}{2} \leq$ result $\leq \dfrac{\pi}{2}$
ACOS(a)	arcosine	$0 \leq$ result $\leq \pi$
ATAN(a)	arctangent	$-\dfrac{\pi}{2} \leq$ result $\leq \dfrac{\pi}{2}$
ATAN(a_1, a_2)	arctangent (a_1/a_2)	$-\pi <$ result $\leq \pi$

Note: Arguments for mathermatical functions must not be INTEGERs.

The output will show the value 3. Such functions are commonly called *intrinsic* or, sometimes, built-in functions since they are part of (built into) the Fortran language. They may be used freely in any arithmetic statement, assignment statement, in relational expressions and in output statements.

```
IF (MOD (N, 2)  .EQ.  0)  THEN
     WRITE (*, *)  'N IS EVEN'
ELSE
     WRITE (*, *)  'N IS ODD'
ENDIF
```

Figure 12.1

The MOD function divides the two arguments and returns the remainder. If N is 13, the result (remainder) becomes 1.

The most commonly used functions are shown in Table 12.1 and have been divided into two categories, arithmetic and mathemetical. Those in the arithmetic class operate on any type of number whilst those in the mathematical class do not operate on integer values!

The arguments of the functions are not restricted to being simple constants and variables. They may be functions themselves, thus:

```
PRINT *,  MAX (REAL (1) , 3.41, REAL (-13) )
PRINT *,  EXP (A*LOG (B) **2) +C
```

Figure 12.2

The one thing to be aware of is that when a function has more than one argument, *all* arguments must be of the same type! Thus:

```
PRINT *,  MAX (4.2, K, L)
```

is illegal, given that K and L are integers. Use the REAL function as shown above.

Here is an example which resolves the well known problem: which is larger, pi ^{e} or e ^{pi} ?

```
      PROGRAM EPI
  COMMENT:   The arctangent of 1 is PI/4

      PI = 4.0*ATAN (1.0)
      IF (PI**EXP (1.0)  . GT.  EXP (1.0) **PI) THEN
          PRINT  *, 'PI TO THE E IS LARGER'
      ELSE
          PRINT *, 'E TO THE PI IS LARGER'
      ENDIF
  C
      PRINT *,
      PRINT *, 'PI TO THE E: ', PI**EXP (1.0)
      PRINT *, 'E TO THE PI: ', EXP (1.0) **PI
      PRINT *,
```

```
C
      PRINT *, 'DIFFERENCE:    ', PI**EXP(1.0) - EXP(1.0)**PI
      END

run

      E TO THE PI IS LARGER

      PI TO THE E:                22.45916
      E TO THE PI:                23.14069

      DIFFERENCE:                -.6815348
```

Figure 12.3

Statement functions

Should a particular function which you would like to use does not exist, then you have no alternative but to write it yourself. If while coding the function it can be written on one line, then you may use the STATEMENT function.

The function must be defined within the program. This definition (your one line of code) must appear before any executable statement and after all other declaration statements (see order of statements in Chapter 15). Another point to note is that all functions are called into action by their *names*, as are subroutines. Thus, the statement function must be given a name, by you.

In a given program, it is required to calculate the following function many times, with the function taking different values for X and Y while A, B, C and D remain constant:

$$ax^2 + by^2 + cxy + d$$

Rather than repeat the computation at each point in the program, we decide to code it once and for all as a statement function, thus:

```
      QUAD(X,Y) = A*X**2 + B*Y**2 + C*X*Y + D
```

This is an example of a statement function which I have called QUAD. It is given the arguments X and Y. On the right of the equals sign I have defined the function ... all on one line. It simply remains for me to use the name QUAD at any point in the executable body of the program:

```
      PROGRAM QUADRT
C        definition of function QUAD
      QUAD(X,Y) A*X**2 + B*Y**2 + C*X*Y + D
C        body of the program
      READ (*,*) A,B,C,D
      READ (*,*) X1, Y1
      PRINT *, QUAD(X1,Y1)
      .................
      .................
      READ (*,*) X2, Y2
      PRINT *, QUAD(X2,Y2)
```

```
         . . . . . . . . . . . . . . . . . . .
         . . . . . . . . . . . . . . . . . .
         READ (*,*) X3, Y3
         PRINT *, QUAD(X3,Y3)
         etc . . . . . . . . . . . . .
```

Figure 12.4

Note that the arguments of the function QUAD within the executable statements are the actual arguments which are passed over to the dummy arguments X and Y in the function definition. The choice of function name is left to the programmer but it cannot be used as a variable or array name elsewhere in the program.

The statement functions, however, are local to the unit in which they are defined. If they need to be used in another unit, they have to be re-defined. It is possible to invoke one statement function from another with mind-boggling effects if taken too far.

```
         PROGRAM AVER
         DIMENSION AVG(25)
         ADDFUN(A,B,C,D) = (A+B+C+D)
         AVGFUN(T1,T2,T3,T4) = ADDFUN(A,B,C,D)/4.0
         OPEN (3, FILE='DATA')
         REWIND(3)
   C       body  of program
   C
         DO 100 I = 1,25
              READ (3,*) S1,S2,S3,S4
              AVG(I) = AVGFUN(S1,S2,S3,S4)
   100  CONTINUE
         . . . . . . . . . . . . . . . . . . . . . . .
```

Figure 12.5

Explanation

The body of the program contains the function name AVGFUN with its arguments S1, S2, S3 and S4 containing values read in from the file DATA. The computer looks back to find the definition of AVGFUN. It now notes that yet another statement function is invoked, namely, ADDFUN. It must now look back for this definition. ADDFUN computes the addition of the dummy arguments A, B, C and D and stores the result in its name ADDFUN.

This result is to be divided by 4.0 and the ensuing result stored in the name AVGFUN. Back in the body of the program, the result of the division is placed in the first element of the array AVG. The DO-loop now forces a second reading of four values from DATA and the function AVGFUN is re-invoked.

> **Question: To what actual arguments do the dummy arguments A, B, C and D refer to?***

*Answer: They refer to S1, S2, S3, S4 read in from 'DATA'.

The sub-program FUNCTION

If we create our own function and in doing so more than one line of code is generated then we have to use the sub-program FUNCTION. This is somewhat like the SUBROUTINE. The function sub-program is created by using the keyword FUNCTION followed by a name. The name is important because it will imply its type.

```
FUN1 = FN(X,Y)
PRINT *, FUN1
. . . . . . . . . . . . .
. . . . . . . . . . . . .
END

FUNCTION FN(A,B)
C  = A**B
D  = C*B
FN = C/D
RETURN
END
```

Figure 12.6

Note that RETURN and END perform the same duties as in subroutines. However, unlike subroutines, FUNCTIONs must always have at least one argument (or a null argument placed in parentheses). The function will always return a value, but only one. If you want a sub-program which returns an array of values, use a SUBROUTINE. The name of the function must appear on the left-hand-side of an equals sign and before any RETURN. This ensures that the name of the function will be assigned a value!

It may be useful to think of the function name as being equivalent to a single memory location into which the single result of the computations performed within the function sub-program is placed. Thus, the result of a FUNCTION is transferred via its name and not via its arguments, as is the case with subroutines.

The name of the function implies its type. Thus, the name 'FN' is real and it will compute a real result. If the name were integer, then integer operations are performed by the function. We can override this first letter type implication by preceding the keyword FUNCTION with the keyword INTEGER or REAL. Thus,

```
INTEGER FUNCTION FN(A,B,C)
```

implies that FN will return an integer value. Functions may be of any type, numeric (real, integer, double precision, complex); logical; and, type character.

Exercises

1. State three differences between functions and subroutines.

2. Write arithmetic statements to compute the values of the following formulae.

(a) $AREA = 2 \cdot P \cdot R \cdot \sin \dfrac{\pi}{P}$

(b) $ARC = 2 \sqrt{Y^2 + \dfrac{4X^2}{3}}$

(c) $s = \dfrac{-\cos^1 x}{x}$

(d) $s = \dfrac{-\cos^{p+1} x}{p+1}$

(e) $g = \dfrac{1}{2} \log \dfrac{1 + \sin x}{1 - \sin x}$

(f) $e = x \arctan \dfrac{x}{a} - \dfrac{a}{2} \log (a^2 + x^2)$

Chapter 13   Characters

Cycle 2

So far our data has consisted of numbers. Let us now see how it is possible to manipulate characters within Fortran 77.

Character constants

A character constant is any group of characters enclosed within single apostrophes. The characters within the apostrophes are sometimes called a *string*. We have been using such strings in WRITE statements when annotating our output. The following are some examples:

```
A = 'THIS IS A CONSTANT'
WRITE (*,*) 'X = '
B = '1 2 3 4, who do we appreciate?'
C = '5678'
```

Figure 13.1

In the last example, '5678' are characters, not the value 5678. We could not perform arithmetic with them. When they are stored in the variable C the apostrophes are not included.

- any character which the computer system supports may be used; we are not restricted to only Fortran 77 characters.

- up to 32767 characters may be entered into a character constant; however, this can vary from machine to machine.

- spaces are significant and must be included when counting the number of characters (called the length of the constant).

Character variables

In the above, the variables A, B and C look like ordinary real variables and, indeed, they are. So character constants cannot be stored in them. What we need to do is to declare those variables to be of type CHARACTER rather than of type *real* which is their default setting. This is done through the CHARACTER statement which needs to be placed after the PROGRAM statement and before the first executable statement.

```
PROGRAM CHAR
CHARACTER * 30 A,B,C,D
A = 'THIS IS A CONSTANT'
etc...
```

Figure 13.2

Now the compiler will establish four memory 'locations' with the names A, B, C and D into each of which 30 characters may be stored. (Depending upon the computer being used, each 'location' will comprise one or more actual memory locations. For example, the CDC CYBER machines can store 10 characters in one memory location. Thus, three locations will need to be reserved for each variable above.)

It is the purpose of the '* 30' in the declaration statement to inform the compiler about the maximum number of characters each variable will contain. It will work out how many actual locations to set aside for each variable. This requires the programmer to count the characters in each constant and can become tedious!

Comparing characters

Characters may be compared within a logical expression in the same way that we compare numbers. Thus, if a sex code of M(ale) or F(emale) were to be read into the character variable SEX, we could determine the number of boys or girls in a given school.

```
CHARACTER * 1 SEX
................
READ (*,*) SEX
IF (SEX .EQ. 'F') THEN
  NG = NG + 1
ELSE
  NB = NB + 1
ENDIF
................
```

Figure 13.3

Note that SEX is compared with the string constant 'F' and that the outcome is either true or false. We could convert the Fahrenheit–Celsius program as follows:

```
PROGRAM TMPCF5
CHARACTER * 1 TYPE
C
C  A program to convert between degrees.
C
DO 100 L = 1,10
READ (*,*) TEMP, TYPE
IF (TYPE .EQ. 'F') THEN
  C = (5.0/9.0)*(TEMP-32)
```

```
          WRITE (*,*) 'CELSIUS = ', C
      ELSE IF (TYPE .EQ. 'C') THEN
          F = (9.0/5.0)*TEMP + 32
          WRITE (*,*) 'FAHRENHEIT = ', F
      ELSE
          PRINT *, 'DATA ERROR, TRY AGAIN! ', TYPE
      ENDIF
100   CONTINUE
      STOP
      END

run
? 'F', -32.0
F = -32.0  C = -35.5556
```

Figure 13.4

When the input prompt (?) is displayed, a character constant has to be input surrounded by apostrophes, that is 'F' or 'C'. This is because the READ statement is in free-format. If we would prefer not to put in the apostrophes, then formatted READ would be required (see Chapter 9) using Aw as the edit descriptor.

Multiple CHARACTER statements

When character variables have different lengths, it is advisable to use multiple CHARACTER statements rather than one. It makes the declarations easier to read. Thus, variables A–F have length 8, except for variable D which has a length of 6.

```
CHARACTER * 8 A,B,C,D * 6,E,F
```

Is it immediately clear that E and F revert back to 8? However, in the following there can be no confusion:

```
CHARACTER * 6 D
CHARACTER * 8 A,B,C,E,F
```

What happens if the lengths differ?

Suppose we have the following:

```
CHARACTER * 4 K,L,M
K = 'THIS'                    K [THIS]
L = 'IS'                      L [IS ]
M = 'ENOUGH'                  M [ENOU]
PRINT *, K,L,M
```

Figure 13.5

We need to know what happens when the declared length differs from the constant length.

There is no problem with K; it is defined as length 4 and is assigned exactly four characters. With L the two characters 'IS' are placed *left* justified with blanks padded out to the right.

In the case of M, the first four characters go in and the last two, 'GH' are lost.

Apostrophes in a constant

Sometimes we may wish to include an apostrophe as part of a constant. To achieve this, it is necessary to use two consecutive apostrophes. For example, the following assignment statement will store DON'T DO IT in location D.

```
CHARACTER * 11 D
D = 'DON''T DO IT'
```

Do not confuse the double single quotes (apostrophes) for the double quote symbol!

Concatentation

It is possible to join together (concatenate) individual character variables using the double slash symbol (//), the division symbol typed twice. However, the character variable which will contain the final result needs to be large enough.

```
     CHARACTER * 4 A,B,C
     CHARACTER * 12 RES
     A = 'THE '
     B = 'TIME'
     C = ' IS:'
     RES = A//B//C
     PRINT *, RES
 output: THE TIME IS:  NOTE: Careful placing of spaces.
```

Figure 13.6

DIMENSIONing CHARACTER variables

Character arrays may be dimensioned in the normal way, using the DIMENSION statement (placed after the CHARACTER type declarative statement), or within the CHARACTER statement itself. Thus, both the following achieve the same effect:

```
CHARACTER * 6 A,B,C,CHAR    CHARACTER * 6 A,B,C,CHAR(4)
DIMENSION CHAR(4)
```

The array CHAR looks like that in Figure 13.7.

Note how easy it is to use up great portions of memory when creating character arrays. The array CHAR (given that two characters may be stored in one memory location) will require:

$(4 \times 6 \text{ characters}) / 2 = 12$ locations.

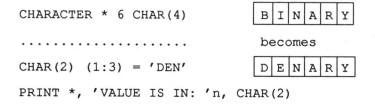

Figure 13.7

We may alter part of a string by an assignment statement. Thus, the following will change the contents of the second element of character array CHAR so that the word 'binary' changes to 'denary':

```
CHARACTER * 6 CHAR(4)

. . . . . . . . . . . . . . . . . . . .

CHAR(2) (1:3) = 'DEN'

PRINT *, 'VALUE IS IN: 'n, CHAR(2)
```

B	I	N	A	R	Y

becomes

D	E	N	A	R	Y

Figure 13.8

The (1 : 3) specifies the starting position and the ending position of the second element of the array CHAR. Thus, characters BIN will be replaced with characters DEN, that is, DEN replaces the first three characters of the second element.

Chapter 14   Further Input and Output Control

Cycle 2

Implied DO-loop

The implied DO-loop provides the programmer with further control over input and output operations. As the name of this feature suggests, it has something to do with the DO-loop and repetition. However, there is a difference between using the implied DO-loop and the DO-loop for repeating input and output. We shall see what this difference is but stress now that the implied DO-loop is used mainly in conjunction with READ and WRITE/PRINT statements.

An example

Let us suppose that there is an array, NARY, with twenty values and that these values are to be printed out. The following does so using a DO-loop:

```
      DO 100 L=1,20
          PRINT *, NARY(L)
  100 CONTINUE
```

Figure 14.1

The twenty values will be printed out, one on each line. This is because the PRINT statement is executed afresh twenty times and each execution forces the next value to be printed on the next line. Even a FORMAT statement, stating that each line should have, say, five values per line will still produce the same result:

```
      DO 100 L=1,20
          WRITE (*,50) NARY(L)
  50      FORMAT (5(I2,3X))
  100 CONTINUE
```

Figure 14.2

However, the implied DO-loop will work:

```
        WRITE (*,50) (NARY(L), L=1,20)      [or, L=1,20,1]
  50    FORMAT (5(I2,3X))
```

Figure 14.3

The implied DO-loop must be enclosed within parentheses. The array and any other variables to be printed are listed in the normal way within parentheses. Above we reference just the array NARY. Note well that the array is separated from the DO-loop counter by a comma.

The above shows L=1,20 and works in the same way as the loop counter in a normal DO-loop, including the increment value. However, the FORMAT statement can specify the output for each line. In the above, five values are printed out on one line with each value separated by three spaces as shown in Figure 14.4.

```
    21    22    23    24    25
    26    27    28    29    30
    31    32    33    34    35
    36    37    38    39    40
```

Figure 14.4

Note that the implied DO-loop of Figure 14.3 does the same as:

```
        PRINT 50, NARY
  50    FORMAT(5(I2,3X))
```

Another example

Let us suppose we have two arrays, A and B, each with six values. We need to display these side by side. This can be achieved with a DO-loop but we use the Implied DO.

```
        WRITE (*,55) (L, A(L), B(L), L=1,6)
  55    FORMAT (5X, I2, 2X, 2(F4.1,5X))
```

```
        A          B                          OUTPUT
    1)  1.2    1)  3.4                 1    1.2    3.4
    2)  2.2    2)  4.4                 2    2.2    4.4
    3)  3.2    3)  5.4                 3    3.2    5.4
    4)  4.2    4)  6.4                 4    4.2    6.4
    5)  5.2    5)  7.4                 5    5.2    7.4
    6)  6.2    6)  8.4                 6    6.2    8.4
```

Figure 14.5

Note that by printing out the subscript, each line of output can be numbered for easy reference!

Two-dimensional arrays

Implied DO-loops may be nested for use with two or more dimensional arrays. Figure 14.6 shows a two-dimensional array, KRAY(1:3,1:4). The following will print out row by row!

```
PRINT *, ((KRAY(L,M), M=1,4), L=1,3)
```

```
run: 1  2  3  4  5
     6  7  8  9 10
    11 12
```

KARY

1	2	3	4
5	6	7	8
9	10	11	12

Figure 14.6

There are several points to notice here:

1. Because there is no FORMAT statement, the computer will print out as many values on one line as it can. Exactly how many will vary from installation to installation. If, in the last line of output, there are fewer values to be printed than in previous lines, this will not cause the computer any problem.

   To print each row with four values on each line, the following FORMAT statement would be required:

   ```
        PRINT 30,  ((KRAY(L,M),M=1,4),L=1,3)
   30   FORMAT (4(I3,2X))
   ```

2. Note the double parentheses at the start of the implied DO-loop. Remember that the *entire* loop must be enclosed within parentheses and, consequently, any inner loop must also be enclosed within parentheses.

> **Warning:** It is advisable always to count the number of opening and closing brackets to ensure that they are the same. If you do not, the compiler will and should the count not be equal, your program will not be executed!

3. The innermost loop is controlled by: M=1, 4. This will be satisfied first. Thus, L remains at 1, while M progresses from 1 through to 4. When M exceeds 4, L is set to 2, and M resumes its progression again 1 through 4.

   To print the array column by column, the two subscripts need to be interchanged, thus:

   ```
        PRINT 35,  ((KRAY(L,M),L=1,3),  M=1,4)
   35   FORMAT (5X, 3(I3,2X))
   ```

READing records

Apart from enabling values to be printed, the implied DO-loop is also used for READing values.

Again, we shall compare the implied DO-loop with the normal DO-loop to illustrate the difference. But first, we digress to discuss record structure.

Record structure

Figure 14.7 shows two data files called NINE and IMPDAT. In NINE there are nine values, three to each line and separated by commas. In IMPDAT there are 15 values held in six lines. Some lines have 1 value, some 2, others 3 and 4!

```
NINE        IMPDAT
1,2,3       1,2,3
4,5,6       4,5,6
7,8,9       7,8,9,10
            11,12
            13,14
            15
```

Figure 14.7

If we attempt to READ six values from IMPDAT via a DO-loop (loop A below), what six values are READ in? Figure 14.8 shows the program and its output for this. The six values READ in are just the first number in each line of IMPDAT. Why is this?

```
        PROGRAM IMP
        DIMENSION NUM(10)
        OPEN(1,FILE='IMPDAT')
        OPEN(2,FILE='NINE')
        REWIND(1)
        REWIND(2)
C           initialise array NUM
        DO 5 I=1,10
            NUM(I) = 0
5       CONTINUE
C
C       LOOP A: attempting to read 1st 6 values!
C
        DO 10 I=1,6
            READ(1,*) NUM(I)
10      CONTINUE
C
        WRITE (*,*) 'HERE ENDS THE DO LOOP. WHAT HAS BEEN READ
                                                        IN?'
        WRITE (*,*)
        WRITE (*,*) (NUM(K),K=1,10)
        WRITE (*,101)
101     FORMAT (//)
C
C       LOOP B:   try again with Implied DO-loop!
C
        READ (1,*) (NUM(K), K=1,6)
        WRITE (*,*) 'IMPLIED DO-LOOP VERSION!'
```

```
      WRITE (*,101)
      WRITE (*,*) (NUM(L), L=1,6)
      WRITE (*,101)
C
C     LOOP C:    read past end of file!
C
      REWIND (1)
      READ (2,*,END=30) (NUM(L), L=1,10)
30    WRITE (*,*) 'EOF ENCOUNTERED. TRANSFER SUCCESSFUL'
      WRITE (*,*) (NUM(L), L=1,10)
      STOP
      END


   run
   HERE ENDS THE DO LOOP. WHAT HAS BEEN READ IN?


   1  4  7  11  13  15  0  0  0  0


   IMPLIED DO-LOOP VERSION!


   1  2  3  4  5  6


   EOF ENCOUNTERED. BUT TRANSFER SUCCESSFUL
   1  2  3  4  5  6  7  8  9  0


   End of Execution
```

Figure 14.8

Because the READ statement is inside a DO-loop, it is repeated exactly six times. Each repetition forces the READ to move onto the next line (called a *record*). Since there is just one variable in the READ statement (the array reference to a single element) this permits only one value to be READ in from the next record. This satisfies the READ statement and the loop is repeated. The READ is executed afresh (moving it onto the next line) and, again, just one value is READ in. In order to read in all values in one line (record), we would need to use either an implied DO-loop or, have sufficient variables in the READ statement.

Since the structure of the file IMPDAT is irregular, that is, the records have anywhere from 1 to 4 values, different READ statements would be required for each record which is different. This would not be possible to organise easily inside one DO-loop!

However, if the implied DO-loop is used, as in Figure 14.8 (loop B), the READ statement is executed once! The implied DO-loop requests six values and also provides the mechanism to supply six elements of the array. Consequently, six values, from records 1 and 2 are READ in.

Loop C reads ten values from file NINE using the END=30 to avoid abortion when the EOF marker is encountered. (See page 86.)

Files/records/fields/items

The entire set of lines or records comprise what is called the *file*. The file IMPDAT, therefore has 6 records, whereas NINE has 3 records. Each record is divided into so many *fields* into which an *item* of data is stored. Thus, NINE has exactly 3 fields in each record. Each field contains an item of numeric data.

It does not usually make sense to vary the number of fields within records because of the necessity to write different READ statements for each record. Consequently, IMPDAT is an example of a poor record structure, whereas NINE with its regular 3 fields per record makes more sense.

Some examples of the implied DO-loop

```
        READ(2,20)  ((A(J,K),J=2,20,2),K=1,30)
        READ(3,30)  (((ITEM(I,J+1,K-2),I=1,25),J=2,N),K=L,M,N)

        DIMENSION VECTOR(3,4,7)
        READ(4,40)  VECTOR  = READ(4,40)(((VECTOR(I,J,K),I=1,3),
  40    FORMAT(I6)             +J=1,4),K=1,7)
```

Figure 14.9

Free-FORMAT or FORMATted?

When creating data files, one should decide in advance whether the READ statement is to be free-FORMAT or FORMATted. Both NINE and IMPDAT are written for free-format since each value is separated by a comma, just like the input from the keyboard. If the READ statement is to be FORMATted, then commas are not allowed, unless care is taken to avoid them! In which case why put them in? Later in this chapter, there is an example of a data structure for use with a FORMAT statement, but first we need to look at some further types of edit descriptors.

E, G and D FORMATS

The edit descriptors met so far have been the Iw and Fw.d for numeric data, nX for spacing and Aw for alphanumeric data. There are three more forms associated with real numbers.

E-format

The possible range of real numbers is enormous, especially for engineering and scientific environments. It would not be sensible if Fortran forced its programmers to type out very small numbers such as: 0.000 000 000 000 000 000 000 024 when 2.4×10^{-23} is the more natural format; or, very large numbers such as: 30 000 000 000.0 when they mean the speed of light in cm per second: 3×10^{10}.

Therefore, a shorthand method using the exponent form is provided. The speed of light in cm per second could be written as: 3.0E10 This is the exponent form which in general is: yEn

where   y is any real number
         E specifies exponent form
         n is any signed integer exponent, thus: $y \times 10^n$.

The following are all real constants written in exponent form:

    + 3.E + 10   2.4E − 23   − 7.2E35   16.35E − 4   .65E10

The exponent form may be used anywhere that a real constant can be used, including keyboard entry and assignment statements:

    BIG = 6.3E15

The symbol E may also appear in FORMAT statements as the following program illustrates.

```
      PROGRAM EFORMAT
 10   WRITE(*,*)'TYPE IN A VALUE FOR X IN FORMAT E13.6 '
      READ(*,990)X
990   FORMAT(E13.6)
      WRITE(*,991)X
991   FORMAT (/'VALUE OF X IN FORMAT  E13.6 IS ',E13.6)
      WRITE(*,992)X
992   FORMAT ('VALUE OF X IN FORMAT  F13.6 IS ',F13.6)
      WRITE(*,993) X
993   FORMAT('VALUE OF X IN FORMAT 1PE13.6 IS ',1PE13.6,/)
      GOTO 10
      END
      run
      TYPE IN A VALUE FOR X IN FORMAT E13.6
      ? 1.23456789e5

      VALUE OF X IN FORMAT  E13.6 IS  .123457E+06
      VALUE OF X IN FORMAT  F13.6 IS 123456.789000
      VALUE OF X IN FORMAT 1PE13.6 IS 1.234568E+05

      TYPE IN A VALUE FOR X IN FORMAT E13.6
      ? 1.23456789e6

      VALUE OF X IN FORMAT  E13.6 IS  .123457E+07
      VALUE OF X IN FORMAT  F13.6 IS ************
      VALUE OF X IN FORMAT 1PE13.6 IS 1.234568E+06

      TYPE IN A VALUE FOR X IN FORMAT E13.6
      ? 3.0000000000.0

      VALUE OF X IN FORMAT  E13.6 IS  .300000E+11
      VALUE OF X IN FORMAT  F13.6 IS ************
      VALUE OF X IN FORMAT 1PE13.6 IS 3.000000E+10
```

```
TYPE IN A VALUE FOR X IN FORMAT E13.6
? +3.e10

VALUE OF X IN FORMAT  E13.6 IS  .300000E+11
VALUE OF X IN FORMAT  F13.6 IS *************
VALUE OF X IN FORMAT 1PE13.6 IS 3.000000E+10

TYPE IN A VALUE FOR X IN FORMAT E13.6
? 2.4e-23

VALUE OF X IN FORMAT  E13.6 IS  .240000E-22
VALUE OF X IN FORMAT  F13.6 IS  .000000
VALUE OF X IN FORMAT 1PE13.6 IS 2.400000E-23

TYPE IN A VALUE FOR X IN FORMAT E13.6
? 0.000000000000000000000024

VALUE OF X IN FORMAT  E13.6 IS  .000000E+00
VALUE OF X IN FORMAT  F13.6 IS   .000000
VALUE OF X IN FORMAT 1PE13.6 IS  .000000E+00
```

Figure 14.10

Note well the last entry!!!!

The w-field specifies the first 13 zeros of the input stream, so zero is printed.

There are two points of interest here. On output, the computer displays the value in a non-standard notation, that is the first significant digit is placed *after* the decimal point! This may be changed by using the so-called scaling factor, P. The P is preceded by a number (either positive or negative) which directs the computer to place the first significant digit ±n places before or after the decimal point. In the above, the 1P asks for the decimal point to be placed one position after the first significant digit.

The second point to notice is that the Ew.d is not exactly the same as the Fw.d. The w specifies the field width (as with Fw.d), but the d specifies the number of significant digits in the entire number. (This does not take a possible scaling factor into account!) We must also allow for the following characters to appear in the E-form: a period, E, + or −, nn. The w must, therefore, exceed the d by at least 5. Seven is said to be a better choice than 5.

Study the different output for the E, F and 1PE formats. Note that the F is not always able to print out the number, hence the rows of asterisks.

G-format

The G-format is similar to the E-format and is called the general format. Basically, if the number can be written without an exponent that is what will appear. If it cannot, then the computer will print out in E-format. The d-field specifies the number of significant digits in either format. The following program illustrates:

```
     PROGRAM GFORMAT
10   WRITE (*,*) 'TYPE IN A VALUE FOR X IN FORMAT G13.6 '
     READ (*,90) X
90   FORMAT (G13.6)
     WRITE (*,91) X
91   FORMAT(/,'VALUE OF X IN FORMAT G13.6 IS ', G13.6)
     WRITE (*,92) X
92   FORMAT ( 'VALUE OF X IN FORMAT F13.6 IS ',F13.6)
     WRITE (*,*)
     WRITE (*,*)
     GOTO 10
     END

     run
     TYPE IN A VALUE FOR X IN FORMAT G13.6
     ? -12345.6789013

     VALUE OF X IN FORMAT G13.6 IS  -12345.7
     VALUE OF X IN FORMAT F13.7 IS -12345.678901

     TYPE IN A VALUE FOR X IN FORMAT G13.6
     ? -123456.78

     VALUE OF X IN FORMAT G13.6 IS  -123457.
     VALUE OF X IN FORMAT F13.6 IS *************

     TYPE IN A VALUE FOR X IN FORMAT G13.6
     ? 1.234e12

     VALUE OF X IN FORMAT G13.6 IS  .123400E+13
     VALUE OF X IN FORMAT F13.6 IS *************
```

Figure 14.11

For those who would like to compare F-format, G-format, E-format and E-format with a scaling factor, the following program may prove useful.

```
     PROGRAM EFGFMT
 10  WRITE(*,*)'TYPE IN A VALUE FOR X IN FORMAT E13.6 '
     READ(*,990)X
990  FORMAT(E13.6)
     WRITE(*,991)X
991  FORMAT (/'VALUE OF X IN FORMAT  E13.6 IS ',E13.6)
     WRITE(*,992)X
992  FORMAT ('VALUE OF X IN FORMAT  F13.6 IS ',F13.6)
     WRITE (*,993) X
993  FORMAT('VALUE OF X IN FORMAT  G13.6 IS ',G13.6)
     WRITE(*,994) X
994  FORMAT('VALUE OF X IN FORMAT 1PE13.6 IS ',1PE13.6,/)
     GOTO 10
     END
```

Figure 14.12

The D-Format

The D-format stands for *double precision* (see Chapter 15, page 127). Here, two locations are set aside for each real number. The second location provides extra significant digits thus increasing the precision of the number after the decimal point.

The general format is Dw.d where the w must be at least five greater than the d. Like the E format, the d specifies the number of significant decimal digits after the decimal point; the w is the total field width for the value itself. This will include the following five characters: decimal point; D to denote double precision; + or – for the exponent; two digits for the exponent itself. The following program illustrates an example.

```
      PROGRAM DOUBLE
      DOUBLE PRECISION A,B
      DOUBLE PRECISION X
      A = 3.1415926535897932D0
      B = 2.0D0
      WRITE (*,*) 'THE VALUE OF B IN FREE-FORMAT IS ',B
      WRITE (*,91) A
91    FORMAT('VALUE OF A IN FORMAT D27.14 IS ',D27.14,/)
      C = A * B
      WRITE (*,*) 'VALUE OF C IN FREE-FORMAT IS ',C
      WRITE (*,92) C
92    FORMAT('VALUE OF C IN FORMAT D27.19 IS ', D27.19)
      WRITE(*,93) C
93    FORMAT('VALUE OF C IN FORMAT D27.21 IS ',D27.21)
      WRITE(*,94) C
94    FORMAT('VALUE OF C IN FORMAT D27.23 IS ', D27.23, '
                                          WHY?', /)
10    WRITE(*,*) 'TYPE IN A VALUE FOR X IN DFORMAT'
      READ(*,95) X
95    FORMAT (D27.22)
      WRITE (*,96) X
96    FORMAT('VALUE OF X READ IN IS ',D38.33,/)
      GOTO 10
      END


      run
      THE VALUE OF B IN FREE-FORMAT IS 2.
      VALUE OF A IN FORMAT D27.14 IS     .31415926535898D+01

      VALUE OF C IN FREE FORMAT IS 6.28318530718
      VALUE OF C IN FORMAT D27.19 IS  .6283185307179564916D+01
      VALUE OF C IN FORMAT D27.21 IS .62831853071795649157D+01
      VALUE OF C IN FORMAT D27.24IS***************************
                                                          WHY?

      TYPE IN A VALUE FOR X IN DFORMAT
      ? 2.34567891234d4
      VALUE OF X READ IN IS
                      .23456789123399999999999999999999122D+05

      TYPE IN A VALUE FOR X IN DFORMAT
```

```
? 2.3d45
VALUE OF X READ IN IS
                    .2299999999999999999999999999999200D+46

End of Execution
```

Figure 14.13

> **WHY?** The format of D27 . 23 does not work since 27-23 = 4 which is not sufficient for the extra *five* characters: D + (or −) . nn!

A data file

Figure 14.14 shows a data file called DATA. It consists of ten main blocks. The first record of each block specifies the number of readings following. Thus the first has 34, others have 50, 20, and so on. The second item in the first record is a temperature in E-format. The rest of the block contains concentration readings which are to be read into an array CONC. Note that these are also in E-format.

Exercises

1. What READ statement would be required to read the first two data items, and what READ statement would be required for the concentrations?

2. The last record is blank (just a blank line) before the EOF marker. How would you detect end of data from this blank line?

> **Detecting End of Data**
>
> **1. Putting in a special end of data marker (page 66).**
>
> **2. Putting END=nnn within the READ statement (page 85f).**
>
> **3. Inserting within the data, the number of values to READ (page 125).**
>
> **4. Inviting the user to enter the number of values to be READ in (page 170).**

```
        34   .60000000E+03
 .26776347E-02   .24472487E-02   .22294366E-02   .20441493E-02   .18629836E-02
 .17100901E-02   .15659884E-02   .14391083E-02   .13134159E-02   .11993812E-02
 .11056875E-02   .10096972E-02   .91987174E-03   .84360594E-03   .77494841E-03
 .70563565E-03   .65186650E-03   .59669225E-03   .54469111E-03   .49984437E-03
 .45429417E-03   .41554984E-03   .38321416E-03   .35066422E-03   .32012746E-03
 .29153849E-03   .26768133E-03   .24615954E-03   .22574709E-03   .20531905E-03
 .18851810E-03   .17313061E-03   .15846834E-03   .14450682E-03
```

```
      22  .61000000E+03
.26340847E-02   .22897116E-02   .19825165E-02   .17156732E-02   .15006345E-02
.12981568E-02   .11296204E-02   .97957732E-03   .85110008E-03   .73774448E-03
.64431117E-03   .55877956E-03   .48472357E-03   .42131812E-03   .36758447E-03
.31707345E-03   .27717519E-03   .23916500E-03   .20922018E-03   .18145365E-03
.15802934E-03   .13651459E-03
      14  .62000000E+03
.25781881E-02   .20667523E-02   .16504541E-02   .13246696E-02   .10646183E-02
.85246887E-03   .68174491E-03   .54419673E-03   .43670515E-03   .34879179E-03
.28139288E-03   .22503511E-03   .18024145E-03   .14423006E-03
      50  .59000000E+03
.27068155E-02   .26010571E-02   .24643545E-02   .23464340E-02   .22397976E-02
.21396346E-02   .20213189E-02   .19349253E-02   .18491209E-02   .17553565E-02
.16644410E-02   .15958994E-02   .15171081E-02   .14405520E-02   .13744929E-02
.13063184E-02   .12491214E-02   .11919215E-02   .11277427E-02   .10782386E-02
.10282146E-02   .98040661E-03   .93346773E-03   .88738465E-03   .84726586E-03
.80550635E-03   .76528885E-03   .73022158E-03   .69824849E-03   .66457140E-03
.62821641E-03   .60350516E-03   .57458414E-03   .54728216E-03   .52041727E-03
.49476398E-03   .46984340E-03   .44744462E-03   .42666899E-03   .40868059E-03
.38640614E-03   .36840553E-03   .35299186E-03   .33669389E-03   .31935947E-03
.30431137E-03   .29029693E-03   .27548874E-03   .26314025E-03   .25029172E-03
etc ..................
      50  .58000000E+03
.27501056E-02   .26713308E-02   .25879907E-02   .24855736E-02   .24039140E-02
.23423114E-02   .22700316E-02   .21933172E-02   .21169466E-02   .20488146E-02
.19911446E-02   .19268670E-02   .18638469E-02   .18005847E-02   .17349118E-02
.16869384E-02   .16341634E-02   .15801524E-02   .15216534E-02   .14791121E-02
.14264119E-02   .13814591E-02   .13411493E-02   .12909960E-02   .12486565E-02
.12132086E-02   .11663562E-02   .11302487E-02   .10923696E-02   .10572570E-02
.10297924E-02   .99441304E-03   .96190296E-03   .92722374E-03   .89964029E-03
.86763778E-03   .84084378E-03   .81965675E-03   .79137918E-03   .76524597E-03
.74290062E-03   .71895789E-03   .69321971E-03   .67032321E-03   .64744141E-03
.62588943E-03   .60778983E-03   .58836708E-03   .56813432E-03   .54993889E-03
.22763417E-02   .22677774E-02   .22593856E-02   .22533036E-02   .22397279E-02
       9  .63000000E+03
.25481794E-02   .17785287E-02   .12567544E-02   .87429641E-03   .61791999E-03
.43053812E-03   .30393225E-03   .21142936E-03   .14935959E-03
       5  .64000000E+03
.24947209E-02   .13572506E-02   .74803910E-03   .40873219E-03   .22123591E-03
```

Figure 14.4

Chapter 15 Further Features

Cycle 3

Further types

Fortran 77 recognises a variety of data types. So far we have met real, integer and character types. There are two more numeric types, namely, double precision and complex, as well as a logical type.

Double precision

The double precision type is an extension of the type real except that the number is stored in *two* memory locations instead of one. This permits the precision of those digits after the decimal point to be extended. However, as with character types, a Double Precision variable must be declared at the start of the program to enable the compiler to reserve two locations for each double precision variable. In other words, in the following, six locations (3 × 2) are required, not three!

```
DOUBLE PRECISION X,Y Z
```

In Chapter 14, we looked at program DOUBLE (Figure 14.13) and saw how to READ and WRITE double precision variables using the Dw.d format. The results from the program were output using a CDC CYBER mainframe. This machine has a 60-bit word (location) which is equivalent to double precision of most other mainframes. Consequently, double precision on the CDC CYBER results in a very high precision number. The maximum field width will vary from machine to machine. I have had occasion to print out a field width of 60 digits on the CYBER, and more were available!

Complex

Unless you need to use complex arithmetic, this type will have little to offer. A complex number consists of two parts, the first being the real part, the second being an imaginary part. Again, this type needs to be declared at the start of the program to enable the compiler to reserve *two* locations for each complex number.

```
COMPLEX X,Y,Z
```

A complex *constant* comprises two real values separated by a comma and surrounded by parentheses: (5.6,2.0)

Arithmetic may be performed on complex numbers and many instrinsic functions are available. A user-defined FUNCTION returning a complex value must also be declared to be of type COMPLEX, thus:

```
COMPLEX FUNCTION CMPLX(X)
```

Figure 15.1 illustrates a program using complex variables.

```
      PROGRAM COMPLEX
      COMPLEX X,Y,PROD,QUOT,SUM,SUBTR,POWER
  10  WRITE(*,*) 'TYPE IN A VALUE FOR X '
      READ (*,910) X
 910  FORMAT(F7.4,F7.4)
C
      WRITE(*,930)
 930  FORMAT(//)
      WRITE(*,*) 'VALUE OF X IS ',X
      WRITE(*,920) X
 920  FORMAT ('REAL PART OF X IS ',F7.4,',   IMAGINARY PART
                                            IS ',F7.4)
C
      Y = (2.0,3.0)
      PROD  = X * Y
      QUOT  = X / Y
      SUM   = X + Y
      SUBTR = X - Y
      POWER = X**2
C
      WRITE(*,*) 'Y IS ',Y
      WRITE(*,*) 'PROD IS ', PROD
      WRITE(*,*) 'QUOT IS ', QUOT
      WRITE(*,*) 'SUM AND DIFFERENCE ARE ',SUM, ' AND ',SUBTR
      WRITE(*,*) 'POWER IS ', POWER
      GOTO 10
      END

 run
    TYPE IN A VALUE FOR X
    ? 12.3456 2.7896
    VALUE OF X IS (12.3456,2.7896)
    REAL PART OF X IS 12.3456, IMAGINARY PART IS 2.7896
    Y IS (2.,3.)
    PROD IS (16.3224,42.616)
    QUOT IS (2.543076923077,-2.419815384615)
    SUM AND DIFFERENCE ARE 14.3456 AND (10.3456,-.2104)
    POWER IS (144.6319712,68.87857152)
```

Figure 15.1

The following shows the rating for each of the numerical types. Note that integer has the lowest; complex the highest

	Integer	Real	Double Precision	Complex
Integer	Integer	Real	Double Precision	Complex
Real	Real	Real	Double Precision	Complex
Double Precision	Double Precision	Double Precision	Double Precision	
Complex	Complex	Complex		Complex

Logical

The final type we look at is the LOGICAL type. It may take one of only two possible values, either TRUE or FALSE. Like the character type, a logical type must be declared at the start of the program:

```
LOGICAL L1, L2
L1 = .TRUE.
L2 = .FALSE.
PRINT *, L1, L2
```
Figure 15.2

When a logical type is printed out, many installations will print either T or F depending upon the value of the logical variable. Logical variables may be assigned logical constants (.TRUE. or .FALSE.) as well as being used in place of a logical expression in an IF statement. This is not so strange as it may appear at first sight. After all, the logical expression is reduced to either TRUE or FALSE, so why not replace a logical expression for a logical variable? It is also possible to assign the outcome of a logical expression to a logical variable. The following illustrates these points.

```
      PROGRAM LOGICAL
      LOGICAL X,Y
      LOGICAL Z,W
      X = .TRUE.
      Y = .FALSE.
      WRITE(*,*) 'VALUE OF X IS ',X, '  VALUE OF Y IS ',Y
      Z = X .AND. Y
      WRITE(*,*) 'VALUE OF Z IS ',Z
      W = X .OR. Y
      WRITE(*,*) 'VALUE OF W IS ', W
10    WRITE(*,99) 'TYPE IN A LOGICAL VALUE FOR X'
99    FORMAT (A,//)
```

```
      READ (*,*) X
      WRITE (*,*) 'X IS NOW ', X
      IF (X) WRITE(*,*) 'X IS TRUE'
      X = 2 .GT. 3
      IF (X) WRITE(*,*) 'X IS NOW TRUE ', '          ', X
      GOTO 10
      END
run
VALUE OF X IS T   VALUE OF Y IS F
VALUE OF Z IS F
VALUE OF W IS T
TYPE IN A LOGICAL VALUE FOR X

? .t
X IS NOW T
X IS TRUE
TYPE IN A LOGICAL VALUE FOR X

? FALSEEE
X IS NOW F
```

Figure 15.3

Note: The input for a logical constant may be in a variety of forms provided (and within reason) that an F or a T appears somewhere. For example: .t .fal faless .f. etc.

The PARAMETER statement

The PARAMETER statement is non-executable. It provides the compiler with certain numeric information which is stored within a PARAMETER variable *before* execution. Each time the parameter variable name is encountered in the program it will be assigned the value established through the PARAMETER statement.

```
      PARAMETER (KDIM=500, NN=1000, ... etc)
      DIMENSION NUMS(KDIM)
      READ (*,*) (NUMS(L), L=1,KDIM)
```

Figure 15.4

Wherever KDIM and NN appear within executable and certain non- executable statements they are 'replaced' by the numeric constants. It is not permitted to alter the value of a PARAMETER variable within the program.

In the above example, the DIMENSION statement has what looks like a variable to state the number of locations to set aside for the array NUMS. This would not normally be accepted. However, since it has previously been declared to be a parameter variable containing the constant 500, the compiler knows how many locations are required. It may help to think of the PARAMETER variable as being a *named constant*.

This feature can be useful where it would be necessary to use the same constant in many places within a program. For example, the maximum number of locations dimensioned for an array seems to be reflected in DO-loops which need to read, write or assign values to the array. If it becomes necessary to increase the dimension of the array at a later stage, all subsequent occurrences within DO-loops and elsewhere need to be changed as well. The more there are, the more likely we are to miss one altogether. However, if we 'parameterise' the constant, just the one PARAMETER statement needs to be altered and we are guaranteed that the changes become effective in all places within the program.

The SAVE statement

Variables within a function or subroutine sub-program which are not in COMMON or in an argument list are *local* to the sub-program. The data in these local variables are lost when control is returned to the calling program. Upon re-entry to the sub-program, the local variables are 'empty'.

> Local variables are those which are local or confined to one sub-program. Global variables are those which can be accessed by any sub-program. Arguments, use of COMMON and BLOCK DATA statements are the major means for establishing global variables.

However, it is possible to preserve the data in one or all of the local variables by use of the SAVE statement provided that it is placed in the relevant routine, together with the list of variables. Upon a subsequent re-entry to the sub-program the data in local variables are preserved. Note that the SAVE statement is meaningless (and has no effect) in the main routine. The following are some valid examples:

```
SAVE                saves all local variables.
SAVE X,Y,Z          saves just X,Y and Z.
SAVE KRAY           saves the array KRAY.
```

See page 133 for an example program.

The ENTRY statement

The ENTRY statement allows a call to a function or subroutine sub-program to begin at a point other than the beginning. There may be more than one entry point. The form of the ENTRY statement is as follows:

            ENTRY name
    or   ENTRY name(argument list)

Program execution begins at the entry point and proceeds until a RETURN is encountered. The following diagram illustrates its use:

```
        CALL XX(A,B,C)  ⟶  SUBROUTINE XX(X,Y,Z)
        . . . . . . . . . . . .       . . . . . . . . . . . . . . . . .
```

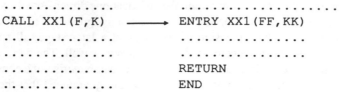

```
. . . . . . . . . . . . . . .           . . . . . . . . . . . . . . . . . .
CALL XX1(F,K)    ─────────▶  ENTRY XX1(FF,KK)
. . . . . . . . . . . . . .              . . . . . . . . . . . . . . .
. . . . . . . . . . . . . .              . . . . . . . . . . . . . . .
. . . . . . . . . . . . . .              RETURN
. . . . . . . . . . . . . .              END
```

Figure 15.5

Another form of RETURN

In Chapter 11 on subroutines, it was stated that the RETURN statement always returned to the instruction after the CALL. In Fortran 77, facilities were added to allow alternate return points. The other points are defined by *n* statement numbers in the argument list of the CALL statement preceded by an asterisk, thus:

```
CALL SUBX(X,Y,Z, *101, *102, *103 ....)
```

This specifies that the first return point is the statement number 101, the second is the statement number 102, etc. The RETURN statement in the subroutine must then be numbered 1, 2, 3, ... n. If a RETURN is not numbered in the subroutine, it will return to the statement after the CALL instruction.

However, the dummy argument list in the subroutine must have asterisks to mark the existence of alternate returns. Figure 15.6 illustrates this.

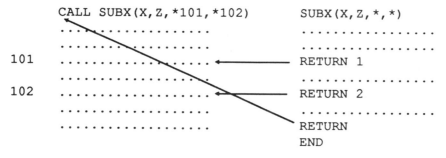

```
CALL SUBX(X,Z,*101,*102)        SUBX(X,Z,*,*)
      . . . . . . . . . . . . . . . .          . . . . . . . . . . . . . . . .
      . . . . . . . . . . . . . . . .          . . . . . . . . . . . . . . . .
101   . . . . . . . . . . . . . . . . ◀─────── RETURN 1
      . . . . . . . . . . . . . . . .          . . . . . . . . . . . . . . . .
102   . . . . . . . . . . . . . . . . ◀─────── RETURN 2
      . . . . . . . . . . . . . . . .          . . . . . . . . . . . . . . . .
      . . . . . . . . . . . . . . . .          RETURN
                                               END
```

Figure 15.6

The DATA statement

There are three different ways to put values into memory cells: the assignment statement, the READ statement and the DATA statement. The first two are executable statements, taking effect during run-time; the last method takes effect during compilation and is, therefore, a non-executable statement. Because of this the DATA statement(s) must precede any executable statement but must follow any specification statement such as DIMENSION. See page 136 for the correct order of declaration statements.

The general form of the DATA statement is:

> DATA namelist/values/namelist2/values/
>
> or
>
> DATA namelist1/values/, namelist2/values/

where: namelistn is a list of variable names, array names, or array elements
         values is a list of the values to be assigned.

An optional comma may be used to separate each set. Furthermore, a value may be repeated by using an integer plus an asterisk in front of the value: 3*2.3

The name list (in full Fortran 77) may be an implied DO-loop. The following are all valid forms of the DATA statement.

```
DATA A,B,I /5.5, 3.5, 9/
```
assigns 5.5 to A; 3.5 to B; 9 to I.

```
DATA B,C(3) /3.5, 9.0/
```
assigns 3.5 to B; 9.0 to C(3).

```
DATA ALPHA /50*0.0/
```
assigns 0.0 to all 50 elements of array ALPHA.

```
DATA (BETA(I), I=11,20)/10*5.0/
```
assigns 5.0 to elements 11–20 of array BETA. Note the use of the Implied DO.

```
DATA (IGAMMA(M,N), M=6,10),N=1,15)/75 * 0/
```
assigns 0 to the last five rows of elements in a 10x15 array.

```
CHARACTER * 5 A,O
LOGICAL TF
DATA A,O /'ALPHA', 'OMEGA'/
DATA TF /.TRUE./
```
assigns ALPHA to A, OMEGA to O.
assigns .TRUE. to TF

Figure 15.7

An example

In this example we bring together an example of the use of the SAVE and DATA statements, and a logical variable. Suppose we need a function which computes the area of a circle given its radius, the function will compute the product of pi and the square of the radius. Therefore, the function will need to know the value of pi. We could type in this value and to the required number of digits which our machine can support. But this would mean looking up a table. Furthermore, if the function were used on another machine with a different accuracy, the constant would have to be re-typed. Why not get each machine to compute pi for itself and to its own internal accuracy?

> pi = 3.14159265358979323846 ...

To do this the function computes pi using the fact that:

pi/4 = arctan(1)

However, each time the function is called, it will compute pi again. To avoid this unnecessary computation, we use a DATA statement to place .TRUE. into a logical variable FLAG. The first time the function is called, it will compute pi and then set FLAG to .FALSE. On every subsequent entry, this flag will prevent pi being computed again. But to keep the orginal computation intact in the variable PI and the value in FLAG we must SAVE their values.

```
        REAL FUNCTION AREA(RADIUS)
        LOGICAL FLAG
        SAVE FLAG, PI
        DATA FLAG /.TRUE./
C
        IF (FLAG) THEN
            PI = ATAN(1.0) * 4.0
            FLAG = .FALSE.
        ENDIF
C
        AREA = PI*RADIUS**2
        RETURN
        END
```

Figure 15.8

INTRINSIC and EXTERNAL statements

There may be occasions when an intrinsic function name, an external function name (one you have created) or a subroutine needs to be used as an actual argument in a subroutine or function call. For example, a CALL statement may wish to specify which of two intrinsic functions, COS or SIN, a subroutine is to use. The subroutine has a dummy argument named AFUNC. This will have to be SIN or COS depending on which is specified in the actual argument list.

The problem is that the compiler cannot distinguish between variable names and function or subroutine names in an actual argument list. It has, therefore, to be told which are function and subroutine names, and not merely user-defined variable names. This is achieved via the INTRINSIC statement, if the function is instrinsic; or, the EXTERNAL statement , if the user has created a function or subroutine sub-program.

```
        PROGRAM XYZ
        INTRINSIC COS, SIN
        .................
        CALL SUBXYZ(A,B,COS)
        .................
        CALL SUBXYZ(A1,B1,SIN)
        .................
        END
```

```
SUBROUTINE SUBXYZ(AA,BB,AFUNC)
.....................
BB = AFUNC(AA)
...................
RETURN
END
```

Figure 15.9

In the above, the first CALL passes the instrinsic function COS for use within subroutine SUBXYZ via the dummy AFUNC. In the second, it passes SIN. Without the INTRINSIC statement in the main routine, the compiler would not know that an instrinsic function was being used in the argument list and would treat COS (later SIN) as a real variable!

Type declaration statements

At the beginning of this book, it was stated that the first letter of a variable or array name indicates its type, thus: I, J, K, L, M and N imply integer; all the other letters of the alphabet imply real. This may be over-ridden by a type declaration statement. Thus:

```
REAL ITYPE, L
INTEGER A,B
```

establishes ITYPE and L to be of type real; A and B to be of type integer. This practice can confuse others who have to read your program and who expect the normal (default) naming convention. This convention is so deeply embedded in the language that to declare an opposite convention for your own personal luxury becomes confusing to others. Therefore, one should use such type statements with caution. Even more so, with the following statement.

The IMPLICIT statement

With this statement, it is also possible to alter the first- letter convention by making all variables with a given first letter a declared type. This is the IMPLICIT statement and must appear before any other specification statement.

```
IMPLICIT INTEGER (A,B), REAL (I-M)
COMPLEX ABLE, BAKER
```

The first statement sets all names with A and B to be of type INTEGER; and all names in the range I-M to be of type REAL. The variable names ABLE and BAKER are defined to be of type COMPLEX even though they begin with letters A and B. This is because all subsequent type declarations over-ride the IMPLICIT statement.

BLOCK DATA sub-program

The term 'sub-program' for the BLOCK DATA is partly a misnomer since it cannot contain any executable statements. The only statements it can include are: DIMENSION, COMMON, EQUIVALENCE, IMPLICIT, SAVE, PARAMETER, TYPE, DATA and the END statement to mark the end of the block.

A BLOCK DATA sub-program may be given an optional name. The reason for the BLOCK DATA sub-program is that named COMMON can be used by several program units but need not be used by the main program. The BLOCK DATA sub-program defines initialisation at the global level of the entire set of programs and sub-programs.

```
SUBROUTINE XX                          BLOCK DATA
COMMON /A/ALPHA(50),BETA,GAM           COMMON /A/ALPHA(50),BETA,GAM
.........................              DATA ALPHA /50*0/, BETA/2.0/
.........................              END
END
```

Figure 15.10

The BLOCK DATA unit initialises ALPHA to zeros, and BETA to 2.0. Note that the COMMON statement in BLOCK DATA must contain all the variable names of the named COMMON (A) even though they are not initialised, such as GAM.

Order of statements

```
PROGRAM (SUBROUTINE, FUNCTION, BLOCK DATA) statement
PARAMETER
IMPLICIT
type statements
other specifications:
  INTRINSIC/EXTERNAL
  DIMENSION
  COMMON/EQUIVALENCE
  SAVE
DATA statements
Statement function
Executable and FORMAT statements
END statement
```

Comment statements may appear anywhere in a program or sub-program. FORMAT statements may appear anywhere within the executable body of a program. We have chosen to put them after the relevant READ/WRITE/PRINT statements. OPEN and REWIND are placed within the executable body of the program.

Appendix A   An Introduction to Program Design

A program design aids the programmer in two main ways. Firstly, it eases the construction of *complex* programs; secondly, it helps the programmer to know when the solution is sufficiently detailed to enable coding to take place.

Complex programs

A complex program is one which is not necessarily complicated but one which contains too many activities for the short-term human memory to cope with at one time. If a program requires more than 5 ± 2 separate activities, then it becomes a candidate for a design. Because of the detailed nature of program instructions, a problem which appears trivial may not prove to be trivial for the short-term memory. Very few people are able to sit down and successfully construct a complex program without some form of plan. Many attempting to do so, fail; taking far more time in debugging their programs than the problem necessitates.

When is it sufficiently detailed?

The process of designing a program involves several levels of design. The programmer needs to begin at a broad level and to refine the design into ever more detailed levels until the final design is a combination of the only operations which a computer can perform. It is then that the programmer should begin to code. There is also a fair chance that the program will contain very few errors (bugs). This approach is called the *top-down* method, and the design itself is often referred to as a *structured diagram*.

Top-down designs

The broadest level simply states the problem, rather like a title for a book. The next level attempts to divide the problem into a series of main steps or sub-tasks, somewhat similar to the chapter headings for a book. The important thing here is to ensure that the sub-tasks are in the correct order, for example, not to process data without first having read it in! Each of these 'headings' can then be taken separately and expanded into more detail. This relieves the programmer from having to concentrate on the whole problem at one time.

It is possible that some sub-tasks may be sufficiently detailed at one level to allow coding to take place, while others require further expansion at lower levels. This is summarised in Figure A.1.

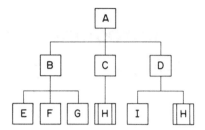

Figure A.1
Hierarchical chart. Note that module H is a recurring module

The diagram shown there is not unlike an up-turned tree with branches stretching downwards. In consequence, this structure is called a *tree structure*. The program designs adopted in this text are much the same except that the tree is turned sideways. Many professional programmers adopt this method, or some similar technique, for their designs.

What are program designs?

Program designs may take one of many forms. In this chapter, the particular method used is one defined, in the late 1970s, for students at Imperial College, London. These designs are based on structured diagrams and may be adapted to suit personal preferences or particular standards adopted at any given organisation.

They make use of brackets and three keywords *repeat, continue* and *exit*.

A bracket is used to identify that what is inside is one identifiable task or function. Initially, if this is at too broad a level, it has to be refined at a lower level into one or more separate brackets, each becoming successively more detailed.

    repeat   is used when a task within one of the brackets has to be repeated–
                      the fundamental reason for using computers.

    continue   is used to indicate that the program continues at the next point in
                      sequence.

    exit (n)   is used to indicate the place of the next instruction to be executed,
                      and where 'n' marks the place.

An example

We take a simple example to familiarise ourselves with the approach to program solutions. Bear in mind that these designs are independent of any particular programming language. A well-constructed design is capable of being coded into *any* programming language using whatever features, structured or unstructured, are available.

The following considers five major steps.

- Problem specification
- The data
- Planning the output
- The design itself
- Test data.

1. Problem specification

It is required to write a program to determine:

a) the average speed for one or more journeys
b) the cost of petrol for each journey.

A journey may involve several trips. In our example, we shall go from point A to point B; point B to point C; point C back to point A; i.e. three trips.

Time is entered in hours, e.g. 2.5 (hours). Assume the car averages 30 miles per gallon. The average speed is found from the following formula:

$$\text{average speed} = \frac{\text{distance covered}}{\text{time taken}}$$

2. The data

Having understood the problem, the next step is to examine the data. The input data consists of:

- the current cost of petrol per gallon, entered as a real value;
- the distances entered as whole (integer) numbers of miles;
- the times entered as real numbers of hours.

The last two will be entered as a pair, distance first, then time, thus: 100 (miles), 2.5 (hours).

The end-of-data marker

There are various ways to inform the program that no more trips are to be entered for a particular journey (see Chapter 14, page 125). One of the simplest is to input an unusual entry for distance and time. When this is encountered, the program 'knows' that no more data is to be entered. Each time an entry is made, the program needs to ask: 'Is this the end-of-data marker?'

If the answer is NO, then it can process the data pair and return to request the input of data for another trip. If the answer is YES, then it does not process this pair and does not return to ask for another entry but continues with the rest of the program.

Since the end-of-data marker has a similiar format to valid data, great care is required in its selection. In our case, each valid data entry consists of an integer value for distance and a real value for time. Therefore, the end-of-data marker must also consist of such a pair. What entry can we use which is so unique that it could never form valid data? One possibility is that of two zeros. Thus, we shall now decide that after the last valid data pair has been input, two zeros indicate that no more trips are to be entered, thus:

150, 2.5	A to B
260, 3.4	B to C
90, 0.5	C to A
0, 0.0	end-of-data marker

3. Planning the output

Since the volume of output is quite small for our program, it may seem unnecessary to go to this trouble. Nevertheless, if we become involved in formatted output (Chapter 9), we will have to specify exact details at some stage. Why not now? We can align columns, see what indentation is most appropriate, what line spacing is required between different results, and so on. It is also a good time to begin to think of possible mnemonics for variable names which will eventually be used in the program. Planning the output also helps to ensure that you understand the problem.

Journey 1:

```
total distance covered:  =    xxxx  miles   (TDIST)
        average speed:   =    xx.xx mph     (AVGSPD)
          petrol cost:   =    xxx.xx        (PETCST)
      at x.xx per gallon
```

Journey 2: if appropriate

End of Trip Costing Program.

The phrases used, 'total distance', 'average speed', etc., can now suggest meaningful variable names, `TDIST`, `AVGSPD`, etc. Such attention to detail, which has to be done at some time or another, helps to ensure that these names will be used only at the correct places in the code. In more complex programs, the programmer will need to make a separate list of each name used, its purpose and any special feature, for example, whether it is a file name, an array, an integer numeric variable, subroutine, and so forth.

4. The design itself

Few of us can begin a design at a sufficient level of detail from which coding could be automatic, that is, where the design statements reflect one of the four fundamental computer operations. Yet this is our goal. Most of us have to begin at a much higher level. The broadest possible level is shown below, where just a name is mentioned, rather like the title for a book. Since every project or program requires a name at some point there is no harm in creating this level.

Level 0: [solve program: TRIP-COST ... TRPCST

Clearly, this is by no means sufficient from which to begin coding and, so, a further level is required. At level 1 the important objective is to list, in the correct order, the major steps in the overall solution, rather like the ordering of chapter headings in a book.

Level 1:

a) ⌈Read in petrol cost
   ⌊Read in distances and times

b) ⌈Calculate average speed
   ⌊Calculate cost of petrol

c) ⌈Output results

d) ⌈Determine if another journey is to be entered.

End of Level 1 Design

Figure A.2

As it stands, level 1 is still not detailed enough from which to code directly into program instructions, and so another level is required. The aim at level 2 is to take each section, one at a time, from level 1 and produce more detail. The advantage of this is that we can now begin to concentrate on *individual* aspects of the total problem, devoting all our concentration and expertise to one task at a time. We do not become distracted by all the other aspects.

One further point is that all programs of any significance become involved in the use of arrays, data files, data types and the initialisation of certain variables. Consequently, we should make a practice of putting these four titles at the start of the level 2 design. As and when we come across names for files, arrays, etc., we can write them alongside the appropriate heading. This ensures that we shall not forget them at the coding stage.

```
Level 2:

┌  ┌FILES:        none
│  │ARRAYS:       none
│  │TYPES:        ANS - character
│ 1)└INIT:        TDIST, TTIME
│ a) ┌   Print:    'Enter cost of petrol per gallon.'
│    │   Input:    cost  ........... PETGAL
│    │
│    │(2) Print:   'Enter distance & time.'
│    │    Input: distance & time     IDIST, TIME
│    │      ┌Is distance & time = 0?
│    │      │   YES ┌EXIT (3)
│    │      │   NO  ┌add distance to total   ... TDIST
│    │      │       │add time to total       ... TTIME
└    └      └       └REPEAT from (2)

│ b) (3) ┌Average speed = tot. dist/tot time
│        └petrol cost = (tot dist/30) * petrol per gallon
│
│ c)     ┌Print: total journey distance   ... TDIST
│        │Print: average speed        ... AVGSPD
│        └Print: petrol cost          ... PETCST
│
│ d)     ┌Print:   'Do you want another go?'
│        │         'Enter Y for yes, anything else means NO'
│        │Input:   answer            ... ANS   (Character)
│        │
│        │ ┌Is answer = 'Y'?
│        │ │
│        │ │   YES ┌REPEAT from (1)
│        │ │
│        │ │   NO  ┌Print: 'End of Trip Costing Program.'
└        └ └       └STOP execution.
```

End of Level 2 Design

Figure A.3

Notes

There are several points worth emphasising:

1. The phrases used in the design, such as: 'petrol cost', 'average speed', 'total time', should suggest mnemonic names for use as variables in the program. It is this level of detail carried out during the design stage that marks the professional from the bungling amateur and saves the former wasting a great deal of time. The list of names used is:

PETGAL	=	cost of petrol per gallon	.. data
PETCST	=	cost of petrol for each trip	.. computed
IDIST	=	distance in miles per trip	.. data
TIME	=	time per trip	.. data
AVGSPD	=	average speed of journey	.. computed
TDIST	=	total distance for journey	.. computed
TTIME	=	total time for journey	.. computed
ANS	=	answer for another go	.. data/character type

2. The four computed variables are candidates for initialisation. If they will appear on the right-hand side of an arithmetic expression before appearing previously on the left-hand-side, they will need to be initialised. This applies to both TDIST and TTIME.

3. No two people are likely to produce exactly the same design. Do not be afraid to let your own creative talents come to the fore. What is presented above is one person's attempt. You may well create 'better' designs.

4. In the finished design, each line is capable of being coded directly into one or more program instructions.

All too frequently, students complain about the length of time spent on writing programs. My first reaction is to ask them to show me their program design to which they invariably confess that they do not have one. Yet, the whole purpose of these designs is to help to write programs. To jump straight into coding without some form of strategy is to court disaster. The outcome of this approach is that an exercise which ought to take an hour or two becomes a chore lasting three or four times as long. It cannot be stressed enough how important it is to put effort into a design. The more that goes into it, the more quickly a complete, working and successful program emerges. It also aids maintenance, as we see below.

5. Test data

The input data consists of a real value for the cost of petrol and trip time, and an integer for distance. All these should be positive. If a negative or zero value were to be entered for any of these, would the program be able to detect the error? As it stands, the answer is NO! It is here that a well-constructed program design proves so useful.

From the design, we can immediately see that there is one natural place to detect data entry errors, that is immediately after the data is input. We now amend our design as follows:

```
(2)       Print: 'Enter cost of petrol per gall.'
          Input: cost … PETGAL
            Is cost negative or zero?
               YES Print: 'Error in petrol cost, try again.'
                   REPEAT from (2)
            NO  CONTINUE
(3)       Print: 'Enter distance & time.'
          Input: distance & time …. IDIST, TIME
            Is distance OR time negative?
               YES Print: 'Error in distance or time, try
                          again.'
            NO  CONTINUE
            Is distance & time = 0?
             etc…….
```

Figure A.4

Our test data should consist of both valid and invalid entries to ensure that the program is robust. The answers will have been worked out in advance, by hand, and compared to those generated by the program. For example:

−1.72	...	cost of petrol (negative and invalid)
1.00	...	cost of petrol (makes it easy to work out)
100, 1.0	...	A to B
50, 0.5	...	B to C
−90, 2.0	...	to test invalid negative distance
90, −.5	...	to test invalid negative time
150, 1.5	...	C to A
0, 0.0	...	end-of-data marker.

Manual results:

    total distance = 300 miles;   total time = 3.00 hours
    average speed = 100 mph (300/3.0)
    petrol cost   = 10.00   (300/30)*1.00

Next steps

The next two steps are to code the program on to paper; finally, to emerge from one's study to find a computer terminal. It is only now that the wise programmer makes bold enough to type in the program. The following is the complete design, code and output results. If the program results are the same as those from the test data, then the program is allowed to run with live/real data.

As an exercise, you may wish to amend the program design to cope with the possibility that someone may enter two zeros as the very first data pair for the trips. As the program stands the results would make no sense. Our test data should have taken this into account and illustrates that the creation of good test data is not a trivial task.

Level 2:

```
    ┌  ┌FILES:    none
    │  │ARRAYS:   none
    │  │TYPES:    ANS - character
    │(1)└INIT: TDIST, TTIME
a) │(2)┌Print:    'Enter cost of petrol per gall.'
    │  │Input:    cost … PETGAL
    │  │
    │  │   Is cost negative or zero?
    │  │
    │  │       YES┌Print: 'Error in petrol cost, try again.'
    │  │          └REPEAT from (2)
    │  │
    │  │       NO ┌CONTINUE
    │  │
    │(3)│Print: 'Enter distance & time.'
    │  │Input: distance & time …. IDIST, TIME
    │  │
    │  │   Is distance OR time negative?
    │  │
    │  │       YES┌Print: 'Error in distance or time, try
    │  │          │                              again.'
    │  │          └
    │  │
    │  │       NO ┌CONTINUE
    │  │
    │  │   Is distance & time = 0?
    │  │
    │  │       YES┌EXIT (4)
    │  │          └
    │  │
    │  │       NO ┌add distance to total    … TDIST
    │  │          │add time to total        … TTIME
    │  └          └REPEAT from (3)
b) │(4)┌Average speed = tot. dist/tot time
    │  └    petrol cost = (tot dist/30) * petrol per gallon
    │
c) │   ┌Print:    total journey distance  … TDIST
    │  │Print:    average speed            … AVGSPD
    │  └Print:    petrol cost              … PETCST
    │
d) │   ┌Print:    'Do you want another go?'
    │  │          'Enter Y for yes, anything else means NO'
    │  │Input:    answer                    … ANS (Character)
    │  │
    │  │   Is answer = 'Y'?
    │  │
    │  │       YES┌REPEAT from (1)
    │  │       NO ┌Print: 'End of Trip Costing Program.'
    └  └          └STOP execution.
```

End of Level 2 Design

Figure A.5

```
      PROGRAM TRPCST
C
C     AUTHOR:     John Shelley
C     VERSION:    1
C     DATE:       12/1/89
C     LANGUAGE:   Fortran 77
C
C     FILES:      none
C     ARRAYS:     none
C     SUBRNTs:    none
C
C     VARIABLES:
C       ANS     character;        Y/N for another journey
C       FLAG    logical;          detects end-of-data, 0,0
C       IDIST   int;              distance for 1 trip
C       KNT     int;              count for invalid entries
C       AVGSPD  real;             average speed of journey
C       PETCST  real;             cost of petrol for journey
C       PETGAL  real;             cost of petrol per gallon
C       TDIST   real;             total distance for journey
C       TIME    real;             time taken for 1 trip
C       TTIME   real;             total time for journey
C
      CHARACTER * 1 ANS
      LOGICAL FLAG
1     FLAG = .FALSE.
      TDIST = 0.0
      TTIME = 0.0
      KNT = 0


C print heading
      PRINT *,'******************************'
      PRINT *,'*                            *'
      PRINT *,'*   COST OF JOURNEY PROGRAM  *'
      PRINT *,'*                            *'
      PRINT *,'*      10 TRIPS MAXIMUM      *'
      PRINT *,'*                            *'
      PRINT *,'******************************'
C
C User allowed 2 invalid entries for petrol cost,
C                         3rd stops program.
C
      DO 100 I = 1,3
         PRINT *, 'ENTER COST OF PETROL PER GALLON'
         READ *, PETGAL
        IF (PETGAL.GT.0.0) GOTO 30
         KNT = KNT + 1
         IF (KNT.EQ.3)  THEN
           PRINT *, '3 INVALID ENTRIES, PROGRAM STOPS.'
           STOP
         ELSE
           PRINT *, 'PETROL CANNOT BE -VE OR 0, TRY AGAIN.'
         ENDIF
100 CONTINUE
C
```

```
C  Maximum 10 trips + end-of-data = 11
C  User allowed 2 invalid entries for distance & time.
C  3rd stops program. DO-Loop requires 13 repetitions.
C
30    KNT = 1
      DO 200 I = 1,13
        IF(FLAG) GOTO 40
        PRINT *, 'ENTER DISTANCE & TIME'
        READ *, IDIST,TIME
C  end-of-data?
      IF (IDIST.EQ.0 .AND. TIME.EQ.0.0) THEN
          FLAG = .TRUE.
C  if +ve
      ELSE IF(IDIST.GT.0 .AND. TIME.GT.0.0) THEN
          TDIST = TDIST + IDIST
          TTIME  =TTIME + TIME
C  if -ve/0
      ELSE IF(IDIST.LE.0 .OR. TIME.LE.0.0) THEN
        IF(KNT.EQ.3) THEN
           PRINT *, '3RD ATTEMPT, PROGRAM STOPS.'
           STOP
        ELSE
          KNT = KNT + 1
          PRINT *, 'DISTANCE OR TIME -VE/0!! TRY AGAIN.'
          PRINT *, 'KNT= ',KNT
        ENDIF
      ELSE
      ENDIF
200  CONTINUE
C
C  now for calculations
C
40    AVGSPD = TDIST/TTIME
      PETCST = (TDIST/30.0)*PETGAL
C
C  now for output
C
      WRITE (*,10) 'TOTAL JOURNEY DISTANCE: ', INT(TDIST),
                                              'MILES'
10    FORMAT (10X,A,I5,A)
      WRITE (*,15) 'AVERAGE SPEED:           ', AVGSPD,' MPH'
15    FORMAT (10X,A,F6.2,A)
      WRITE (*,15) 'COST OF PETROL:          ', PETCST
      WRITE (*,20) 'AT ',PETGAL,' PER GALLON.'
20    FORMAT (10X,A,F4.2,A,//,)
C
C  determine whether another go required
C
300  PRINT 25, 'DO YOU WANT ANOTHER JOURNEY?   (Y/N)'
25    FORMAT (A)
      READ 25, ANS
      IF (ANS.NE.'Y' .AND. ANS.NE.'N')GOTO 300
      IF (ANS .EQ. 'N') THEN
          PRINT *, 'END OF TRIP COSTING PROGRAM.'
          STOP
      ENDIF
```

```
GOTO 1
END
```

Figure A.6

Notes

1. A maximum of ten trips are allowed plus end-of-data. This gives 11 reads. However, 3 invalid entries are allowed, thus the maximum number of reads is $10 + 1 + 2 = 13$. If 3 invalid entries are made, the loop stops the program.

2. The logical FLAG is introduced to prevent using a GOTO jumping backwards and within an IF...THEN...ELSE construction. However, a backward GOTO is used for invalid Y/N entries since the loop is close to the GOTO. Also it is more simple to code.

Appendix B   Structured Programming

A good program has certain qualities, some of which are:

- that it works! i.e. it solves correctly the problem for which it was written.
- that it is robust, i.e. it does not fail no matter what idiotic thing the user inputs.
- that it is easy to read.
- that it is easy to maintain, i.e. even though the original programmer is no longer around, someone else may make changes with comparative ease.

There is a high probability of achieving all four if the program is *well structured*. What then is a well-structured program? Obviously, it has something to do with 'structured programming'.

The birth of the structured programming movement

It has been mentioned on several occasions now that the uncontrolled use of the GOTO is considered 'harmful' since the logic of the program, that is, which instruction to execute next, tends to become confusing so that the program resembles a bowl of spaghetti. We see the end of one piece but have no idea where the other end is. Pulling at one end has unseen repercussions on other pieces. This point was brought to the attention of the programming fraternity by Edsger Dijkstra, in 1968, in a letter to the Editor of the *Communications of the ACM*, entitled, 'Go to Statement Considered Harmful'*, wherein he wrote:

'For a number of years I have been familiar with the observation that the quality of programmers is a decreasing function of the density of go to statements in programs they produce... I became convinced that the go to statement should be abolished from all 'higher level' programming languages...'

What is important about this letter is that, being one of the Great Men of Computing, Dijkstra's voice was powerful enough to be heard by many, in many countries. Those who read the letter, will find that he was not merely stating that he found the GOTO to be harmful but that he gave a good explanation of why it was harmful.

However, the inherent danger of the GOTO was well known to many ALGOL programmers years before and formulated in an article by Naur, in 1963.† There, he made the point that intelligent use of constructs such as IF...THEN...ELSE and FOR...DO, make for clearer

---

* C.ACM Vol. 11, No. 3, March, pp. 147f
† *Comp. J.* Vol. 5, 1652/63, pp. 349–67.

programs than the unrestricted use of GOTOs and labels. Perhaps, this is a better reference for the dawn of the structured programming movement.

The actual term *structured programming* dates from the publication of a book by that title in 1972.* Since that time, the term has become widely used and, depending on context, has different meanings. For our purpose, I borrow from Schnieder, Weingart and Perlman:†

> 'Although structured programming does not yet have a fixed definition, its most important concerns are for the types of control statements needed in a programming language and the relationship between certain control structures and a program's clarity.'

It now remains for us to look at what the authors mean by *control statements* and *control structures*, and why these are needed in programming languages.

Structured programs

It is too simple to say that a structured program is one that contains few (or no) GOTOs. However, this is at the heart of the matter, to reduce or eliminate the GOTO. Before we can appreciate this, we need to be aware that programs consist of three essential processes or activities. (This was proved by Bohm and Jacopini.‡)

- sequence (and concatenation)
- choice
- repetition.

Program processes

Sequence

It has already been mentioned that, at the simplest level a program is executed in strict sequence, that is, when one operation is completed, the flow of control passes on to the next instruction in sequence. This is illustrated in Figure B.1. Note that the operation in one box may involve one instruction (such as an input/output statement, an arithmetic statement, etc.), or, indeed, a group of instructions in the form of a sub-program (a subroutine or function).

Once the sub-program is completed, control is RETURNed to the next instruction after the invoking statement, thus preserving the concept of sequential execution. Some find this form of sequence so important that they call it *concatenation*.

---

* Dahl, Dijkstra and Hoare, *Structured Programming*, Academic Press, 1972.

† *An Introduction to Programming and Problem Solving with Pascal*, 2nd edn, John Wiley & Sons, 1982.

‡ C. ACM No. 5, May 1966, pp. 366–71.

The sequence structure is represented by two process symbols:

Each process box represents an operation; the flow of control is from one operation to the next. For example:

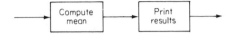

One frequent use of the sequence structure is to represent a sub-routine or sub-program. For example:

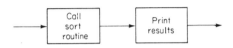

Figure B.1
Sequence

It is then sometimes known as concatenation.

Choice

When choice is involved, one of two situations may occur:

 either: the choice involves two and only two selections
 or: the choice involves more than two selections.

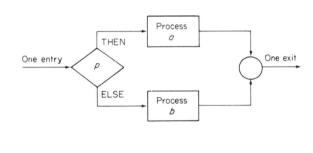

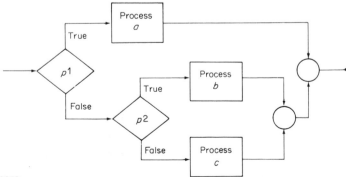

Figure B.2
Choice, two or more

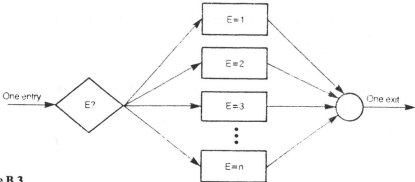

Figure B.3
Another choice process using CASE

Both these are represented by the diagrams in Figures B.2 and B.3. Some of the early high-level languages could realise these situations only by the use of the simple conditional branch instruction, for example, the logical IF in Fortran IV. This positively encouraged the use of the GOTO. Since Dijkstra's letter, however, interest in features which could eliminate the GOTO has been fermenting. Today, we have the structured IF...THEN...ELSE and the CASE statements.

The IF...THEN...ELSE has been discussed fully in Chapter 6 where it was additionally mentioned that the multiple IF...THEN...ELSE IF could be used when more than two selections were involved. However, it is the CASE statement which is specially designed for many choices, but it does not form part of Fortran 77's repertoire.

The CASE statement

Figure B.3 shows the classic diagram for CASE. It is particularly useful for menu-driven programs. A menu of choices is printed out and the user is invited to select one. This selection is stored in a variable name (CHOICE is used below) and used within the CASE statement.

```
CASE
     of CHOICE = 1 DO choice1
     of CHOICE = 2 DO choice2
     ......................
     of CHOICE = n DO choicen
ENDCASE
```

Figure B.4

If the choice is 2, choice 1 and the others are ignored. The 'DO choice 2' is typically a call to a sub-program. On completion of the choice 2 sub-program, control is usually passed to the statement following the ENDCASE. However, each language has its own specific syntax and idiosyncrasies which need to be understood before using CASE.

Repetition

Figures B.5, B.6 and B.7 show the three classic diagrams for repetition. They illustrate each of the three possible situations which can arise:

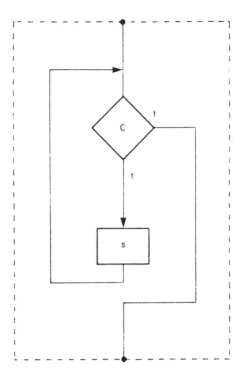

Figure B.5
The repetition process using DOWHILE

- the exact number of repetitions is known
- the exact number of repetitions is not known but:
    a) at least one repetition will be involved
    b) even one repetition may not be involved.

Of the three, the DO...WHILE is paramount, that is the number of repetitions is unknown and even one repetition of the loop may not be required. This is achieved by testing for the condition *before* entering the loop. While the condition holds true, the loop is repeated. While it does not hold true (i.e. is false) the loop is abandoned, even on the first test.

The REPEAT...UNTIL allows at least one pass through the loop simply because the condition to repeat the loop is placed at the end. The loop is repeated until the condition proves true.

The FOR...NEXT in BASIC (the DO-loop in Fortran, FOR..DO in Pascal) has been discussed fully in Chapters 6 and 8.

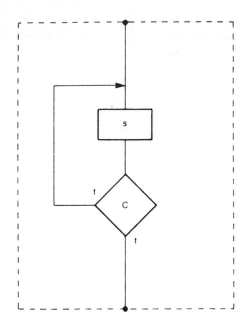

Figure B.6
Another repetition process using REPEATUNTIL

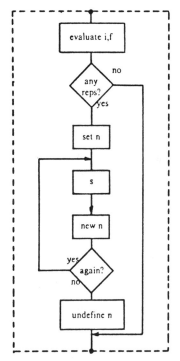

Figure B.7
Another repetition process using FORNEXT

Of the three, Fortran has the DO-loop alone. But by placing a logical IF statement as the first executable instruction in the DO-loop coupled with a GOTO (to an instruction outside of the loop), the DO...WHILE can be implemented.

```
      DO 100 I=1,200
         IF(X.LT.998.0) GOTO 210
         .....................
         .....................
100   CONTINUE
210   CONTINUE
```

Figure B.8

Some support for GOTO

The poor old GOTO has taken a battering since the publication of Dijkstra's famous letter. His advice, when taken seriously, certainly leads to better-quality programs. But, as with any movement, extreme positions are adopted. The more extreme members of the structured programming movement claim that *any* use of the GOTO is inherently wrong. Yet, there are situations when the use of the GOTO is the most natural and clearest method to use.

Let us say at once that these situations are usually exceptional and should involve a *forward* jump rather than a backward one which is by definition a loop and better expressed by use of one of the structured repetition features. One such example is the use of the logical IF to exit a DO-loop before the number of repetitions has been exhausted.

> It is interesting to note that the dBASEIII programming language has no GOTO. It has the IF...THEN...ELSE, the DO...WHILE and the CASE features, as well as the equivalent of Fortran's subroutine. These features result in clear, well-structured programs.

Well-structured programs

The characteristics that a well structured program exhibits are:

- few, if any GOTOs, achieved by use of structured features
- it is easy to read and the logic flows from top to bottom instead of jumping here, there and everywhere. This means that the program is read from top to bottom like ordinary text
- it is easy to maintain because additional instructions may be inserted without major disturbance to the rest of the program, and existing code can be changed and the effect of such changes easily identified
- when the program is tested and errors found, the bugs are more easily discovered and corrected.

When we also make use of:

- meaningful variable names
- indentations
- using variables for only one purpose
- making proper use of comments within the program listing
- preferring clear code to clever tricks

then the well-structured program becomes a professional piece of work.

Appendix C   Answers to Selected Problems and Further Examples

Answers to selected problems

1. c) Columns 73–80. Also, columns 2–80 if C appears in column 1.

2. No, it may begin anywhere within columns 7–72.

4. The colon (:).

6. If it immediately precedes the END statement.

7. 6 characters.

8. & } o and b (lower case not allowed) " ! ? ; \ (wrong way round)

Chapter 4

1. To mark the end of the data typed in (the input stream) and to send this data to the computer's memory.

2.
1003 integer and valid]   1,324 [invalid, no commas]
0.0 [real and valid]   303.123 [real and valid]
0.032,567,890 [invalid, no commas]
−87.512.62 [invalid, double periods]
+ 0012.67 [real and valid]   .7654 [real and valid]
0 [integer and valid]

6.
COST.	invalid, period not allowed
INT1	integer and valid
R3	real and valid
SAVINGS	invalid, seven characters
JOB NO	integer and valid. Spaces ignored
Kt	invalid, lower case not allowed
2ABCD	invalid, first character not alphabetic
X7V56Y	real and valid, but not meaningful!
TYPE 2	real and valid
−GTF	invalid, first character not alphabetic
K9	integer and valid
INK	integer and valid.

9. Nothing, they both achieve the same result.

10. There is only one apostrophe in Fortran and it must be used at either end.

11. Missing R in PROGRAM. Program name exceeds 6 characters. C of Comment not in column 1. No comma between variable names. Double quotes not a Fortran character. END comes before STOP and vice versa.

Chapter 5: Cycle 1

4. The assignment statement merely assigns a constant (or contents of a variable) to the left-hand-side variable. The arithmetic statement computes a value for the left-hand side.

5. X still retains 3.45; Y will contain 4.65.

7. Integer 10, truncation takes place.

8. The secret is to create a temporary variable, thus:
```
TEMP = A
A = B
B = TEMP
```

9.
```
a)    (A+B)/(C+D)
b)    ((A+B)/(C+D))**2 + X**2
c)    (A+B)/(C+(D/(E+F)))
d)    1.0+X+X**2/2.0+X**3/6.0
e)    (X/Y)**(G-1.0)
f)    ((A/B)-1.0)/(G*((G/D)-1.0))
```

Figure C.1

Chapter 5: Cycle 2

1. (a) is wrong. (b) and (c) are both correct. I prefer (c) because it does not invoke mixed mode arithmetic and is easier to understand.

2.
```
X = SQRT(Y)
X = SQRT(Y+B)
X = ABS(Y-B)
X = EXP(Y+B)
X = (A/B +2)**(1.0/3.0)
X = SQRT(ABS(Y+5.0))
```

Figure C.2

Chapter 6: Cycle 1

1. (P.GT.X)   (Y.GT.2.5)   (I.EQ.J)
   (J.NE.99)   (K.GE.L2)   (C.LE.D)

2.
```
IF (N.EQ.3) THEN
     N2=0
ELSE IF (N.EQ.1) THEN
     N2=3
ELSE IF (N.EQ.2) THEN
     N2=3
ELSE
     PRINT *, 'N IS NOT 1,2 OR 3.'
ENDIF
```

or after Cycle 2:

```
IF (N.EQ.3) THEN
     N2=0
ELSE IF (N.EQ.1 .OR. N.EQ.2) THEN
     N2=3
ELSE
     PRINT *, 'N IS NOT 1,2 OR 3.'
ENDIF
```

Figure C.3

3. Since Y is not initialised and has not been given a value via an assignment statement or a READ statement, we cannot know what value it contains.

Chapter 6: Cycle 2

1. (K.LT.L .AND. K.GT.M)   (M.EQ.J .OR. M.GT.6*7)
   (R.EQ.D .AND. F.NE.T .OR. W.LT.F)

4. (i) Encourages use of GOTO. (ii) Only one instruction may be executed when the logical expression is true.

5. The statement after the logical expression *and* the instruction on the next line will be executed.

6.
```
            PROGRAM DESIGN for PROGRAM ROOTS2

      ┌PRINT 'To stop program, enter 3 zeros'
   (1)│PRINT 'Enter 3 values, separated by commas'
      │
      │INPUT three values        ...... A,B,C
      │
      └Are values = 0?
```

```
┌YES  ┌PRINT 'End of Program Message'
│     └STOP execution
│ NO  ┌Calculate expression to be squared
│     │Is expression negative?
│     │              YES  ┌PRINT 'No Real Roots'
│     │                   └Repeat from (1)
│     │              NO   ┌Calculate roots
│     │                   │Print results
└     └                   └Repeat from (1)
```

End of Design

Figure C.4

Chapter 6: Cycle 3

2. Simply because it is within an inner set of parentheses.

Chapter 7: Cycle 1

1. A(-3) invalid in Fortran IV, no negative subscripts allowed.
    MANNO(5.0) invalid, subscripts cannot be real.
    AREA(MINIMUM) invalid, subscript has more than 6 characters.
    JOB NO(1 0) valid, spaces ignored.

2. STORE = ALIST(10)

3. TEMP = A(3)
    A(3) = A(4)
    A(4) = TEMP

4. X(I) = A(I)*B(I)

6. In Fortran, arrays are always established by the compiler during the compilation stage and not during run-time.

Chapter 7: Cycle 2

4. PRINT *, MATXYZ(2,3)

5. DIMENSION MATXYZ(3,4) or DIMENSION MATXYZ(1:3,1:4)

6. X has 7 Y has 20 K has 11 × 6

7. X has no positive and no zero subscripts.
    Y a subscript does not use a colon, only DIMENSIONs.
    K has no negative column reference.

Chapter 8: Cycle 1

3. The default is set to 1.

5. Array A is set to 20 but the DO-loop will attempt to read 30 values. The 21st read will encounter the end-of-file marker.

Chapter 8: Cycle 2

1. Via a GOTO statement!

3. True.

5. Manipulation of arrays of two or more dimensions.

6. (i) Used as a subscript. ii) To count number of times the DO-loop has been repeated.

Chapter 9: Cycle 2

1. I5 in the READ statement is an integer variable name; I5 in the FORMAT statement is an edit descriptor.

2. (a)   PRINT 50,
   50 FORMAT (5X,'HEADING A',10X,'HEADING B',10X,'HEADING C')
   (b)   WRITE (*,15) A,B,C
   15 FORMAT (7X,3(F10.3,3X))

3. (a) LL contains 123, JJ contains 78901, KK contains 12
   (b) LL and MM will require their own input stream. LL cannot pick up any value left over from the previous input stream.

4. Either in the FORMAT statement itself, or within the WRITE/PRINT statement provided that an Aw edit descriptor is used in the FORMAT.

Chapter 10: Cycle 1

2. The system will CLOSE the file for us.

3. The file associated with unit 3 will not be kept. Its data will be lost and the space it took up can be given to another file.

Chapter 12: Cycle 2

1. (i) Subroutines need not have an argument, a function must always have at least one. (ii) Subroutines may return any number of results, a function can return but one. (iii) A single

CALL statement activates a subroutine; the function is used in an assignment statement. (iv) There is no type implication in a subroutine name, but the name implies the type of result returned by a function.

2. (a) `AREA = 2.0*P*R*SIN(3.141593/P)`
    (b) `ARC = 2.0*SQRT(Y**2+1.333333*X**2)`
    (c) `S = -COS(X)**4/X`
    (d) `S = -COS(X)**(P+1.0)/(P+1.0)`
    (e) `G = 0.5*ALOG((1.0+SIN(X))/(1.0-SIN(X)))`
    (f) `E = X*ATAN(X/A) - (A/2.0)*ALOG(A**2+X**2)`

Figure C.5

Chapter 14: Cycle 2

1. There are two leading blanks before each record, thus:

```
      READ (*,50) N,TEMP
 50   FORMAT (I10,E15.8)
      ................
      READ (*,55) (CONC(I),I=1,N)
 55   FORMAT (5(E15.8))
```

Figure C.6

2. The last record is blank (just a blank line) before EOF. The READ into N and TEMP will read in two zeros. N can be tested for zero to determine the end of data.

Solutions to program exercises

4.1.
```
      PROGRAM RDWRT
C     Program Exercise 4.1.
C     a program to read 2 reals & 2 integers
C     and to output these values.
C
      WRITE (*,*) 'ENTER 2 INTEGERS'
      WRITE (*,*) '& 2 REALS'
      WRITE (*,*) 'EACH SEPARATED BY A COMMA.'
      READ (*,*)  INT1, INT2
      READ (*,*)  REAL1, REAL2
      PRINT *,
      PRINT *, 'THE 2 REALS ARE:    ', REAL1,REAL2
      PRINT *, 'THE 2 INTEGERS ARE: ', INT1,INT2
      END
```

Figure C.7

5.1.

```
        PROGRAM AVRAGE
        PRINT *, 'ENTER 3 +VE REAL VALUES'
        READ *, A,B,C
        SUM = A+B+C
        AVER = SUM/3.0
        PRINT *, 'VALUES READ IN: ',A,B,C
        PRINT *, 'SUM     = ', SUM
        PRINT *, 'AVERAGE = ', AVER
        END
```

Figure C.8

5.3.

```
        PROGRAM CHARGE
        PRINT *, 'ENTER PRICE OF 3 ITEMS.'
        READ *, P1,P2,P3
        TOTCST = P1+P2+P3
        VAT    = TOTCST*0.15
        AMOUNT = TOTCST+VAT
        PRINT *, 'TOTAL COST = ', TOTCST
        PRINT *, 'PLUS VAT   = ', AMOUNT
        END
```

Figure C.9

5.4.

```
        PROGRAM TRIANG
        PRINT *, 'ENTER THE 3 SIDES'
        READ (*,*) A,B,C
        S = (A+B+C)/2.0
        AREA = SQRT(S*(S-A)*(S-B)*(S-C))
        PRINT *, 'AREA = ', AREA
        STOP
        END
```

Figure C.10

6.1.

```
        PROGRAM ARITH2
  C
  C     DETECTS -VE COST AND/OR PERCENTAGE
  C     MAKES USE OF .OR. SEE CYCLE 2
  C
        WRITE (*,*) 'ENTER COST & DISCOUNT (AS A
                                  PERCENTAGE)'
        READ (*,*) COST, PERCNT
        IF (COST.LT.0.0 .OR. PERCNT.LT.0.0) THEN
            PRINT *, 'CANNOT HAVE -VE COST/PERCNT'
            STOP
        ELSE
            CONTINUE
        ENDIF
        DISCNT = COST*(PERCNT/100.0)
```

```
            AMOUNT = (COST-DISCNT)*0/15
            WRITE (*,*)
            WRITE (*,*) 'CHARGE + VAT = ', AMOUNT
            END
```

Figure C.11

6.2.
```
      PROGRAM TRIANG
C
C DETECTS IMPOSSIBLE SIDES OF A TRIANGLE
C
      PRINT *, 'ENTER THE 3 SIDES'
      READ (*,*) A,B,C
      S = (A+B+C)/2.0
      HALFP = S*(S-A)*(S-B)*(S-C)
      IF(HALFP.LT.).)) THEN
          PRINT *, 'SIDES CANNOT MAKE A TRIANGLE'
          STOP
      ELSE
          AREA = SQRT(S*(S-A)*(S-B)*(S-C))
          PRINT *, 'AREA = ', AREA
      ENDIF
      END
```

Figure C.12

8.1.
```
      PROGRAM AVER2
C NOTE THAT THE INPUT & OUTPUT WILL BE MIXED TOGETHER.
C TO OUTPUT ALL VALUES AFTER INPUT WOULD REQUIRE AN ARRAY.
C
      TOTAL = 0.0
      DO 100 I=1,6
          READ *, NUM
          PRINT *, NUM
          TOTAL = TOTAL+NUM
  100 CONTINUE
      AVER = TOTAL/6.0
      PRINT *,
      PRINT *, 'TOTAL   = ',TOTAL
      PRINT *, 'AVERAGE = ',AVER
      END
```

Figure C.13

8.2.
```
      PROGRAM AVER3
      DIMENSION ANUM(6)
      TOTAL = 0.0
      DO 100 L=1,6
          READ *, ANUM(L)
          TOTAL = TOTAL+ANUM(L)
  100 CONTINUE
```

```
      AVER = TOTAL/6.0
C
C now print out values
C
      DO 200 L=1,6
          PRINT *, ANUM(L)
200  CONTINUE
      PRINT *,
      PRINT *, 'TOTAL   = ',TOTAL
      PRINT *, 'AVERAGE = ',AVER
      DO 300 L=1,6
          IF (ANUM(L).LT.AVER) THEN
              PRINT *, ANUM(L)
          ENDIF
300  CONTINUE
      END
```

Figure C.14

8.4. We need to amend the first DO-Loop as follows and to increase the array ANUM to some unreachable maximum. COUNT will keep track of the number of repetitions, i.e. numbers read in.

```
      DIMENSION ANUM(10000)
      TOTAL = 0.0
      COUNT = 0
      PRINT *, 'ENTER  ZERO TO STOP INPUT
      DO 100 L=1,10000
          READ *, ANUM(L)
          IF (ANUM(L).EQ.0.0) GOTO 60
          TOTAL = TOTAL+ANUM(L)
          COUNT = COUNT+1
100  CONTINUE
60   AVER = TOTAL/COUNT
      etc
```

Figure C.15

8.5.
```
      PROGRAM ROWCOL
      DIMENSION N(3,4)
C
C     first the rows
C
      DO 110 L=1,3
          TOTROW = 0.0
          DO 100 M=1,4
              TOTROW = TOTROW+N(L,M)
100       CONTINUE
      PRINT *, 'ROW ',L,' = ',TOTROW
110  CONTINUE
C
C   now for the cols
C
```

```
      DO 210 M=1,4
         TOTCOL = 0.0
         DO 200 L=1,3
            TOTCOL = TOTCOL+N(L,M)
 200     CONTINUE
      PRINT *, 'COL ',M,' = ',TOTCOL
 210  CONTINUE
      END
```

Figure C.16

9.1.

```
      DO 200 L=1,6
         PRINT 30, 'VALUES READ IN'
 30      FORMAT (7X,A)
         PRINT 32, ANUM(L)
 32      FORMAT (10X,F6.2)
 200 CONTINUE
      PRINT 34,
 34  FORMAT (//)
      PRINT 36, 'TOTAL   = ',TOTAL
 36  FORMAT (7X,A,F8.2)
      PRINT 36, 'AVERAGE = ',AVER
      DO 300 L=1,6
         IF (ANUM(L).LT.AVER) THEN
            PRINT 38,
 38         FORMAT (7X,'NUMBERS LESS THAN AVERAGE')
            PRINT 40, ANUM(L)
 40         FORMAT (11X,F5.2)
         ENDIF
 300 CONTINUE
```

Figure C.17

10.1.

```
      PROGRAM IOEXER
      DIMENSION ANUM(10)
      OPEN(4,FILE='DATA1')
      REWIND(4)
 C   create data file using RANF
      DO 100 I=1,10
         AN = RANF()*10.0
         WRITE (4,*) AN
 100 CONTINUE
 C   rewind 4 and read into array ANUM
      SUM = 0.0
      PRINT *, 'VALUES READ IN'
      DO 200 I=1,10
         READ (4,*) ANUM(I)
         SUM = ANUM(I)+SUM
         PRINT *, ANUM(I)
 200 CONTINUE
 C   compute average and print out values and results.
      AVER = SUM/10.0
      PRINT *, 'TOTAL   = ', SUM
```

```
      PRINT *, 'AVERAGE = ', AVER
      END
```

Figure C.18

11.1.
```
      PROGRAM TMPCNV
      DO 100 L = 1,10
          PRINT *, 'ENTER TEMPERATURE & TYPE'
          PRINT *, '2 ZEROES STOP THE PROGRAM.'
          PRINT *,
          READ (*,*) TEMP, ITYPE
          IF (ITYPE .EQ. 1) THEN
              CALL CELCON(TEMP)
          ELSE IF (ITYPE.EQ.2) THEN
              CALL FAHCON(TEMP)
          ELSE IF (ITYPE.EQ.0) THEN
              PRINT *, 'STOP CHOSEN'
              STOP
          ELSE
              PRINT *, 'INVALID ENTRY: ',ITYPE
          ENDIF
  100 CONTINUE
      END

      SUBROUTINE CELCON(XTEMP)
C
C convert to Celsius
C
      C = (5.0/9.0)*(XTEMP-32)
      WRITE (*,*) 'CELSIUS = ',C,'FAHRENHEIT = ',XTEMP
      RETURN
      END

      SUBROUTINE FAHCON(XTEMP)
C
C convert to Fahrenheit
C
      F = (9.0/5.0)*XTEMP + 32
      WRITE (*,*) 'FAHRENHEIT = ',F,'CELSIUS = ',XTEMP
      RETURN
      END
```

Figure C.19

Additional exercises

1. Using RANF ( ), generate 20 integer numbers in the range 11–30 and store them in array NUM. Invite the user to enter a value in range 11–30. Search array for the value input and print out the subscript if found, or message 'Not Found' if not found.

Note use of logical FLAG to detect a match.

```
      PROGRAM ADDEX1
      LOGICAL FLAG
      DIMENSION NUM(20)
      DO 100 I = 1,20
          NUM(I)  = RANF()*20.0+11.00
100   CONTINUE
C
10    PRINT *, 'NOW ENTER VALUE TO SEARCH FOR'
      PRINT *, 'IN RANGE 11-30. 0 STOPS PROGRAM.'
      READ *,  IVALUE
      IF(IVALUE .EQ. 0) STOP
      FLAG = .TRUE.
C
      DO 200 I = 1,20
          IF(NUM(I) .EQ. IVALUE) THEN
              INDEX = I
              FLAG  = .FALSE.
          ENDIF
          IF(.NOT.(FLAG)) GOTO 30
200   CONTINUE
C
30    IF (FLAG) THEN
          PRINT *, 'VALUE: ',IVALUE,' NOT FOUND.'
      ELSE
          PRINT *, 'VALUE: ',IVALUE, ' AT INDEX: ',INDEX
      ENDIF
      GOTO 10
      END
```

Figure C.20

2. Write a program to print the interest accumulated in a bank account over x years, with an initial deposit of x pounds and an interest rate of x%. Allow the user to enter the period of years (IYRS), the initial deposit (DEP) and the interest rate (RATE).

```
      PROGRAM BNKACN
C
C CALCULATE INTEREST RATE
C
      PRINT *, 'ENTER INTEREST RATE, PRINCIPAL, PERIOD OF YEARS'
      READ *, RATE, DEP, IYRS
      PERCNT = RATE*100.0
      PRINT 50, 'YEAR    TOTAL @: ', PERCNT,'%'
50    FORMAT (9X,A,F5.2,A)
      WRITE (*,55)
55    FORMAT(/)
      IPER = 0
      DO 100 I = 1,IYRS+1
          PRINT 60, IPER,DEP
60        FORMAT (10X,I3,5X,F9.2)
          DEP = DEP+DEP*RATE
          IPER = IPER+1
100   CONTINUE
      PRINT 55
      PRINT *, 'END OF PROGRAM.'
      END
```

Figure C.21

3. Write a subroutine which will interchange rows and columns of square matrices. The subroutine should be capable of handling matrices from 2×2 to 20×20.

```
      CALL MOVE (ARRAY, IRWCOL)
      . . . . . . . . . . . . . . . . . . . .
      SUBROUTINE MOVE (A, IRC)
C
C     A is the dummy array.
C     IRC the number of rows & cols.
C
      DIMENSION A(20,20)
      DO 110 I = 1, IRC
         L = I+1
         DO 100 J=L, IRC
            TEMP = B(I,J)
            B(I,J) = B(J,I)
            B(J,I) = TEMP
110      CONTINUE
100   CONTINUE
      RETURN
      END
```

Figure C.22

4. The best straight line ($Y = mX + c$) through a number of experimental points (X, Y) can be obtained by using linear regression. This method relies on the square of the errors between the points and the best straight line being minimised. The value of m in the above equation is given by the following:

$$m = \frac{\sum X_n Y_n - \dfrac{\sum X_n \sum Y_n}{N}}{\sum X_n^2 - \dfrac{\left(\sum X_n\right)^2}{N}}$$

and c, the intercept, by:

$$c = \frac{\sum Y_n - m \sum X_n}{n}$$

Write a program to calculate the values of m and c from a number of X and Y data points (at least 6) which you have made up on approximately a straight line (not an exact straight line), for example:

X	Y
1.0	1.1
2.0	1.9
3.1	3.1
4.0	4.5
5.0	4.7
6.0	5.9

The answer for the above data is: slope(m) $= 0.97$

intercept(c) $= 0.13$

```
PROGRAM DESIGN:

LEVEL 0:[solve LINREG problem

LEVEL 1:

    determine number of data points

    read in all values

    calculate equation

    output: heading for X & Y
            values of all X & Y
            m & c

    determine if another go required

LEVEL 2:
    files: none
    subroutines: none
    arrays:      X & Y  ... upto 10!
    initialised variables:  SUMX, SUMY, SUMXY, SUMX2

(1)  Print: How many entries?
     Input: number of entries        .... N

     Input: all values for X & Y, as pairs

     Calculate equation    ... leave till Level 3!

     Print:  Heading for X & Y
             Values for X & Y
             m & c

     Print:  Do you want another go?   1 for Yes, 0 for No.
     Input: answer        .... ISTPGO

       Is ISTPGO = 0?

         YES Print: end of program message
             STOP execution
         NO  Repeat from (1)

End of Level 2.

Level 3: Just the calculation.
     calculate: sum of all X * all Y   SUMXY
                sum of all X    ... SUMX
                sum of all Y    ... SUMY
                sum of all X **2       ... SUMX2
     calculate:  m
                 c

End of Level 3 & Design
```

Figure C.23

```
      PROGRAM LINREG
      DIMENSION X(10), Y(10)
      SUMX  = 0.0
      SUMY  = 0.0
      SUMXY = 0.0
      SUMX2 = 0.0
1     WRITE (*,*) 'HOW MANY ENTRIES REQUIRED?'
      READ (*,*) N
      DO 10 I = 1,N
          READ (*,*) X(I), Y(I)
10    CONTINUE
C
C DO PARTIAL SUMS
C
      DO 20 I1=1,N
          SUMX  = SUMX + X(I1)
          SUMY  = SUMY + Y(I1)
          SUMXY = SUMXY+(X(I1) * Y(I1))
          SUMX2 = SUMX2+ (X(I1)**2.)
20    CONTINUE
C
      AN = N
      AM = (SUMXY - (SUMX*SUMY/AN))/(SUMX2 - (SUMX**2.0/AN))
      C  = (SUMY - (AM*SUMX)) / AN
      WRITE (*,100)
100   FORMAT (10X,'X',8X,'Y')
      DO 30 I2 = 1,N
          WRITE (*,101) X(I2), Y(I2)
101       FORMAT(8X, F4.1,5X,F4.1)
30    CONTINUE
      WRITE (*,102)
102   FORMAT(///)
      WRITE (*,103) AM,C
103    FORMAT(3X,'SLOPE = ',F6.2,/,3X,'INTERCEPT = ',F6.2)
C
      WRITE (*,*) 'ENTER 1 FOR ANOTHER GO, 0 TO STOP'
      READ   (*,*) IGOSTP
      IF (IGOSTP .EQ. 0) THEN
          WRITE (*,*) 'END OF LINEAR REGRESSION PROGRAM.'
          STOP
      ELSE
      ENDIF
      GOTO 1
      END
```

Figure C.24

5. Write a subroutine which will sort an array of integer values into ascending order. The main program should print out the unsorted array and the sorted array. In the following, the subroutine counts the number of comparisons (NCOMPS) and the number of swaps (NSWAPS) and prints these out. It may be of interest to appreciate just how hard a sort routine has to work.

There are a variety of sort routines already available as subroutines in Fortran. The one used here is called a *bubble sort*. It assumes that the first in the array is the largest and compares this with the next in the array. If the next is less, the values are swapped around. Each time a swap takes place, a flag is set (NSWFLG = 1). It continues with all the other elements in the same way.

The only time the routine knows that the values are in the correct order is when it makes a complete pass through the array *without* making any swaps. Hence the purpose of the variable NSWFLG. Note that it has to be re-set to zero prior to each pass through the DO-loop.

```
      PROGRAM SORTS
      DIMENSION NUM(100)
C
      DO 100 L=1,100
          NUM(L) = RANF()*100.0+1.0
100   CONTINUE
C
      PRINT 50, (NUMS(I), I=1,100)
50    FORMAT (15X,'UNSORTED ARRAY',//,6(5X,I5))
      CALL SORT(NUM, NSWAPS, NCOMPS)
      PRINT *, 'COMPARISIONS = ', NCOMPS
      PRINT *, 'SWAPS       =', NSWAPS
      PRINT 55, (NUMS(I), I=1,100)
55    FORMAT (15X,'SORTED ARRAY',//,6(5X,I5))
      END

      SUBROUTINE SORT(NNUMS,NSWPS,NCPMS)
      DIMENSION NNUMS(100)
      NSWPS = 0
      NCPMS = 0
10    NSWFLG = 0
      DO 200 I=1,100
          IF(NNUMS(I).GT.NNUMS(I+1)) THEN
              TEMP = NNUMS(I)
              NNUMS(I) = NNUMS(I+1)
              NNUMS(I+1) = TEMP
              NSWFLG = 1
              NSWPS = NSWPS+1
          ELSE
          ENDIF
      NCPMS = NCPMS+1
200   CONTINUE
      IF (NSWFLG.EQ.0) RETURN
      GOTO 10
      END
```

Figure C.25

What would happen if the relational operator in SORT were changed to .GE. instead of .GT. and two values in the list were equal?

Catastrophe! The program would loop forever. This should make us be careful and diligent when using relational operators.

6. Standard deviation program: real values, 1.0–50.0.

```
      PROGRAM STDEV
      DIMENSION X(200)
C
C THIS PROGRAM GIVES THE STANDARD DEVIATION FOR A SET OF
C VALUES UPTO 200 MAXIMUM
10    PRINT *, 'ENTER NUMBER OF VALUES, 0 STOPS PROGRAM'
      READ *, NN
C     DETECT END OF PROGRAM RUN
            IF (NN.EQ.0) THEN
            WRITE (*,*) '0 ENTERED, PROGRAM STOPS'
            STOP
            ENDIF
C
      PRINT *, 'ENTER SEED - WHOLE,ODD & REAL'
      READ *, Y
      CALL RANSET(Y)
C
      DO 100 I=1,NN
            X(I) = 50*RANF()+1.0
100   CONTINUE
      CALL STANDV(X,NN)
      GOTO 10
      END
      SUBROUTINE STANDV(XX,N)
      DIMENSION XX(200)
      SUMX=0.0
      XSQ =0.0
      XSUMSQ =0.0
      DO 100 K=1,N
            AN = N
            SUMX=SUMX+XX(K)
            XSQ = XSQ+XX(K)**2.0
100   CONTINUE
C
      WRITE (*,50) 'VALUES ARE'
50    FORMAT(10X,A,/)
      WRITE (*,55) (XX(I), I=1,N)
55    FORMAT(5(F9.2,2X))
C
      PRINT 60, SUMX,XSQ
60    FORMAT(/,5X,'SUM OF X: ',F8.2, '   X^2: ',F10.2)
C
      AMEAN = SUMX/AN
      XSUMX = SUMX*SUMX
      STDV = SQRT(AN*XSQ-XSUMX)
      WRITE (*,62) AMEAN,STDV
62    FORMAT(//,'MEAN IS: ',F6.2,'STANDARD DEV. IS: ',F10.3)
C
      XSUMSQ = SUMX**2
      WRITE (*,65) XSUMSQ
65    FORMAT(/,'SUM OF X^2 IS: ',F12.2)
      RETURN
      END
```

Figure C.26

Glossary of Terms

Here is a list of jargon words and acronyms used in this text.

absolute address – the actual and physical address of a store location in central memory as determined by the hardware.

algorithm – a series of instructions or steps which define the solution of a problem.

arithmetic/logic unit – ALU, that part of the CPU which performs arithmetic and logic operations.

argument – a value in a variable name used by a sub-program.

array – a set of consecutive storage locations referenced by a single name. Individual elements are referenced by adding a subscript to the name.

ASCII – American Standard Code for Information Interchange. It refers to a particular combination of binary patterns used to represent characters in a computer. Many manufacturers use their own codes, peculiar to their own machines, but a number of standard codes are used to facilitate the transmission of data between computers.

assembler – a program which converts programs written in assembly code instructions into the machine code of a given computer.

assignment – placing the value of one variable or constant into another variable.

auxiliary storage – any type of storage media other than the central memory. Usually, refers to magnetic tape and magnetic disc.

balanced parentheses – the same number of opening and closing brackets.

binary digits – the two digits, zero and one, as used in the binary number system.

bit – one of the binary digits.

bounds (of an array) – the upper and lower values a subscript may take as defined in the DIMENSION statement.

bug – a mythical creature which is believed to exist in computer programs when they do not work. The process of correcting a program is called "debugging". The mistakes are, of course, due to our own shortcomings as programmers, but it is comforting to blame something else.

byte – a group of eight bits. Characters are often stored as one byte.

carriage control character – a special character required by *line* printers and which provides information about the movement of the paper.

central memory – the main memory of the CPU. Program instructions and data are held in this unit. Sometimes called the *immediate access store*.

central processing unit – or CPU, consists of the essential electronics which perform the processing of data.

character set – the complete set of characters which can be represented and processed by a particular computer. Each programming language tends to have a set of characters which are the only ones used when writing instructions in that language. In Fortran 77, there are the 26 capital letters of the alphabet; the ten digits 0 to 9; + (plus symbol); – (minus symbol); * (asterisk); / (solidus); , (comma); . (period); : (colon); $ (dollar sign); () (open and close parentheses); = (equal sign); 'space', and ' (single quote or apostrophe).

coding – the writing of instructions in a given computer programming language.

compilation – the process of compiling source code into object code.

compiler – a program which converts (translates) program instructions written in a high-level language into the machine code of a given computer.

computer – originally any person or machine capable of processing numbers. Today, it refers to the complete set of hardware and software which can accept information, process that information and produce results.

conditional branch instruction – departure from the normal sequential execution of program instructions to some other instruction. The jump to this other instruction is dependent on the result of some test.

constant – a fixed data item (either numeric or character) in a program instruction.

control unit – the CU is that part of the CPU which supervises the execution of program instructions.

data – information coded and structured in a form acceptable for input to, and processing by, a computer system.

diagnostic error message – a message attempting to indicate the type of error in a program. Diagnostics are produced by the compiler during translations or by the computer system during run-time.

direct access – see *files.*

disc – a circular piece of magnetic material capable of storing computer-readable information on a permanent basis.

EBCDIC – Extended Binary Coded Decimal Interchange Code; one of several standard codes to facilitate the exchange of data between computer systems.

end-of-data marker – a special data item placed after valid data so as to identify the end of the valid data to be processed.

execution –the carrying out of instructions specified by a computer program.

file – an organised collection of related records. It is also a term used to cover the storing of information, either data or program instructions, as an entity within the computer's permanent storage system.

In Fortran 77, records in a file may be read or written in one of two ways, either sequentially or randomly (directly). In sequential mode, records are written to a file one after the other, thus: record 1, record 2, record 3, ... record *n*. They can be read only in the same order. Therefore, if one specific record is required, all preceding records must be read first. In a sequential file, all records must be either all formatted or all unformatted. The last record is a special formatted *endoffile* which informs the computer that the end of the file has been reached. The records, however, need not be of the same length.

In contrast, in a direct or random file containing *records*, records may be read or written in any order by reference to a record number (which must be a positive number in the range 1 to *n*. In a direct access file, records must be all of the same type (i.e. formatted or unformatted) and must be of the same length.

floating-point – a form of notation in which numbers are expressed as a fractional value (mantissa followed by an integer exponent of the base). It is used to increase the range of numbers which can be stored in a computer memory location.

hardcopy – computer output printed on paper.

hardware – the visible parts of a computer which can be touched.

index (of a array) – sometimes called a *subscript.* It is used to locate an individual element of an array,

infinite loop – a loop without a means of exit and, thereby, causing the instructions in the loop to be repeated indefinitely.

instruction – a request for a computer to perform some given operation. The term *statement* is sometimes used when a given instruction is more concerned with informing the computer of a particular situation; for example, to 'call' a subroutine into action and to supply relevant information about arguments.

integer – a numerical value without a decimal point.

interactive programming – a program designed to allow the computer and the program user to communicate with each other during the execution of the program.

interpreter – a translator program of a high-level language which translates and immediately executes one program statement at a time.

keyword – (also *reserved word*) used here to mean those special words used as part of the vocabulary of a programming language; for example, READ, DO, IF, etc. They should not be used as variable names within a program.

line printer – a special and expensive printer which prints one whole line at a time. Contrasted with the character printer which prints one character at a time in succession (cf. the typewriter). The two are frequently, but incorrectly, confused.

listing – the printing out in sequence of program instructions or data.

location – the basic unit within a computer's main memory unit which is capable of storing a program instruction or data item(s).

logical operator – One of the keywords indicating a logical operation: OR, NOT, AND.

log-off – the act of disconnecting a terminal from contact with the computer system.

log-on – the act of connecting a terminal to a computer system.

loop – (also *jump, branch*): a sequence of instructions which is to be executed repeatedly until some specified (hopefully) condition is satisfied.

machine-code instruction – an instruction in such a form that it can be immediately interpreted by the electronic circuits in a computer without the need for any intermediate translation.

object code – the translated version of a program which has been compiled.

operating system – a set of programs which 'drives' the computers' hardware system and provides for the support and execution of users' programs.

operators – a term used in programming to mean those symbols used to indicate arithmetical, relational (comparison) and logical operations.

parameter – (also *arguments*): a name or value made available to a sub-program (e.g. subroutines and functions) from a calling program, or vice versa.

portability – a term used to describe the situation whereby a program (or certain hardware, such as disc drives) may be used without alteration on more than one make of computer.

program – a complete set of program instructions arranged in such a way as to complete a given task or problem.

program design – used here to indicate a particular method of describing the steps which are necessary to achieve the solution for a given problem.

program logic – used here to refer to which one of two possible courses of action to follow as determined by the outcome of a specified test.

punch card – high-quality cards which have holes punched in them to represent our everyday information. Fortran was originally designed to be used with punch cards. The standard card has 80 columns. In Fortran: columns 1–5 were used for statement numbers, if column 1 had a C punched, the rest of the card was considered to be a comment within the program. Column 6 was used as a continuation of the previous card if anything other than blank or zero was punched in it. Columns 7–72 (inclusive) were used for the Fortran statement itself. Columns 73–80 (inclusive) were used by the programmer as a field for his or her own purpose and was not part of the Fortran statement.

range checks – checks made by a program to see that data lies within some acceptable range. For example, the age of school children must lie between 4 years and 18 (possibly 19) years.

real – a numerical value with a decimal point.

sequential access – see *files*.

source code – the program written by a programmer. It will need to be translated into an object code version.

string – a combination of characters treated as text. In Fortran the string must be enclosed in single quotes.

subscript – see *index*.

syntax – the set of rules for combining the elements of a given programming language into permitted constructions. When the rules are broken, a *syntax error* has been made.

systems analysis – a vague term used to describe everything a systems analyst must perform, with the exception of actually writing programs, in order to computerise a particular application. It will include an analysis of the requirements of a job; the feasibility study of potential computer involvement; and the detailed design of an appropriate system to do the job.

systems programmer – a programmer who specialises in the writing of computer system software.

test data – data specified by a programmer (or systems analyst) to test a program. The expected results are worked out beforehand and compared with those produced by the program.

trace – a means of checking the logic of a program by inserting statements which cause the values of suspect variables or other information to be printed out as the program is in execution. A trace program is part of the computer's software which can perform this task automatically for such features as subscripts, DO-loop counters, etc.

trip counts – the number of times a DO-loop is executed according to the loop counter's values.

unbalanced parentheses – a term used when the number of opening parentheses does not match the number of closing parentheses, or vice versa.

unconditional branch instruction – an instruction, such as GOTO, which causes departure from the normal sequential execution of program instructions but without any condition attached. It may, therefore, cause an infinite loop. It is disliked by computer program theoreticians since the excessive use of GOTOs results in highly unstructured programs.

variable – a name (called an *identifier* in programming) used within a program to allow the programmer to associate the name with a particular storage location.

VDU – visual display unit. A device with keyboard entry for information and display screen for output.

word – another term for a storage location.

word length – the number of binary digits a word contains.

Index